INTERVENTION

KEN HUDNALL
OMEGA PRESS
EL PASO, TEXAS

INTERVENTION

COPYRIGHT © 2018 KEN HUDNALL

All rights reserved. No part of the book may be reproduced or transmitted in any form or by any means, graphic, electronic, or mechanical, including photocopying, recording, taping or by any information storage or retrieval system, without the permission in writing of the author.

OMEGA PRESS

http://www.kenhudnall.com

FIRST EDITION

Printed in the United States of America

OTHER WORKS BY THE SAME AUTHOR UNDER THE NAME KEN HUDNALL FROM OMEGA PRESS

MANHATTAN CONSPIRACY SERIES
Blood on the Apple
Capitol Crimes
Angel of Death
Confrontation

THE OCCULT CONNECTION
UFOs, Secret Societies and Ancient Gods
The Hidden Race
Flying Saucers
UFOs and the Supernatural
UFOs and Secret Societies
UFOs and Ancient Gods
Evidence of Alien Contact
Intervention
Secrets of Dulce
Unidentified Flying Objects
Sensual Alien Encounters
Strange Creatures From Time and Space
Beyond Roswell
Alien Encounters
Mysteries of Space
Battle of Los Angeles
Is Someone On The Moon?

DARKNESS
When Darkness Falls
Fear the Darkness

SPIRITS OF THE BORDER
(with Connie Wang)

INTERVENTION

The History and Mystery of El Paso Del Norte
The History and Mystery of fort Bliss, Texas

(with Sharon Hudnall)
The History and Mystery of the Rio Grande
The History and Mystery of New Mexico
The History and Mystery of the Lone Star State
The History and Mystery of Arizona
The History and Mystery of Tombstone, AZ
The History and Mystery of Colorado
Echoes of the Past
El Paso: A City of Secrets
Tales From the Nightshift
The History and Mystery of Sin City
The History and Mystery of Concordia
The History and Mystery of ASARCO
Military Ghosts
School Spirits
Restless spirits
Railroad Ghosts
Nautical Ghosts
Haunted Hotels
Haunted Hotels in Arizona and Colorado
Ghosts of Albuquerque
The History and Mystery of Tucson
The History and Mystery of Santa Fe

SHADOW WARS
The Shadow Rulers
The Secret Elite

THE ESTATE SALE MURDERS
Dead Man's Diary
A Bloody Afternoon of Fun

BOOK OF SECRETS

Ancient Secrets
Secrets of the Dark Web

Northwood Conspiracy

No Safe Haven: Homeland Insecurity

Where No Car Has Gone Before

Seventy Years and No Losses: The History of the Sun Bowl

How Not To Get Published

Lost Cities and Hidden Tunnels Along the Border

Vampires, Werewolves and Things That Go Bump in The Night

Border Escapades of Billy the Kid

Criminal law for the Layman

Understanding Business Law

Language of the Law

Death of Innocence: The Life and Death of Vince Foster

The Veterans' Practice Primer

Why Would They Say It?

PUBLISHED BY PAJA BOOKS
The Occult Connection: Unidentified Flying Objects

PUBLISHED BY PRUNE DANISH PRESS
Why Would They Say It?

DEDICATION

As with all of my endeavors, this would not be possible without the support and assistance of my lovely wife, Sharon Hudnall.

TABLE OF CONTENTS

WHAT IS AN INTERVENTION? 11

UNEXPLAINED ADVANCES 21

ANOTHER NEW BEGINNING 33

HOME OF THE GODS 55

THE GODS ORGANIZE THEIR SERVANTS 59

THE GODS GO TO WAR 77

THE END OF THE OLD ORDER 89

STRANGE AIRSHIPS 93

MYSTERIOUS AERIAL ATTACKS 109

AN EARTH-SHATTERING KNOWLEDGE 127

OTHER SIGHTINGS 139

THE BATTLE OF LOS ANGELES 147

INCIDENTS WITH FOO FIGHTERS 163

NAVAL ENCOUNTERS 177

THE GHOST ROCKETS 185

OPERATION HIGH JUMP 189

THE COLD WAR YEARS 197

THE SECRECY 207

INDEX 213

CHAPTER ONE
WHAT IS AN INTERVENTION?

The word intervention is defined as interference by a country in another country's affairs. In other words, someone from the outside interfering with the actions of a group. This interference can be positive or negative. It can help the group or interfere with the group. The intent does not matter. What matters are the actions.

Well, for any student of history it is eminently clear that the activities of both this nation as well as the human race as a whole have been interfered with, both in a positive way as well as a negative way. In this work, we will present evidence that some of this interference has come from outside the human race.

There is more and more evidence supporting the idea that the UFO presence on this planet predated the human race, or at least the current Homo Sapien based human race.

Speaking of Homo Sapiens, let us look at Zecharia Sitchin's work, The 12th Planet[1]. In the first chapter of this marvelous work he asks two very valid questions about life on this Planet.

- *If life began here through a series of spontaneous chemical reactions, why does life on Earth have but a single source, and not a multitude of chance sources?*
- *Why does all living matter on Earth contain too little of the chemical elements that abound on Earth and too much of those that are rare on our planet?*

This goes along with a question I heard on a television show not too long ago. If man descended form

---

[1] Sitchin, Zecharia, The 12th Planet, Bear & Company, Rochester, Vt. And Toronto, Canada, 1976.

ape, why are there still apes? It would seem that, assuming that apes were the dominate form at the time something led one or more apes to become Homo Sapiens, that some outside force affect some apes and not others. Such a random concept presupposes that this radical change in gene makeup of some apes that led to Homo Sapiens, happened to some and not all apes. How could this be?

Then there is the time that these wonderous changes came about. When this author was in high school, many moons ago, science taught that man originated in Africa some 500,000 years ago[2]. The first mother was known as Lucy. Of course, this dating was based on finding a skull here and a jaw there and interpolating the available data to come up with a theory[3] and a date.

Even religion got involved in the game of determining when man was created. According to

---

[2] Ibid
[3] It must be remembered that even Darwin's Theory of Evolution is just that, a theory that has never been proven, however, science treats everything Darwin said as if it were the word of God.

Archbishop Ussher[4], creation took place at 6:00 PM. on Saturday October 24, 4004 BC. He arrived at this date based on information contained in the King James Bible.

When asked about the fossil records that predate this time period, he claimed that they were fakes created to try and draw men from the path of righteousness. While he was clearly a brilliant man, his reasons left something to be desired. In fact, my own family history proves his theory incorrect as records regarding my ancestors predate 4004 BCE.

CREATION OF MAN

Current scientific research has shown that evolution generally moves slowly. Assuming that man did descend from the ape[5], these apelike ancestors are now dated to

---

[4] Archbishop James Ussher was a seventh century Anglican cleric and biblical scholar who used data contained in the Scriptures to determine that God created the world on October 23, 404 BCE. He wrote this in a 1658 chronology entitled The Annals of the World.

[5] Frankly, the actions of some of my fellow writers does tend to confirm this theory.

25,000,000 years ago[6]. More recent discoveries coming out of East Africa tend to show that the transition to what might be referred to as manlike apes happened about 14,000,000 years ago and the first so called ape-man that might fit the classification of *Homo*[7] was thought to have happened about 3,000,000 years ago.

The first truly manlike creature, referred to as "Advanced Australopithecus" came out of the same parts of Africa about 2,000,000 years ago. About one million years ago, came Homo Erectus. Then roughly 100,000 years ago came Neanderthal, not truly human, but certainly closely related to Homo Sapiens.

---

[6] Sitchin, Zecharia, The 12th Planet, Bear & Company, Rochester, Vt. And Toronto, Canada, 1976.

[7] For those whose mind immediately descended to the gutter, this term is Latin for human being. Homo is the genus that encompasses the extant species Homo Sapiens plus several other species that were classified as either ancestral or closely related to humans.

FATE OF THE NEANDERTHAL

There are many questions regarding what happened to this cousin of Homo Sapien. Early research tended to discount the very idea that Neanderthal and Homo Sapien may have interbred. However, new DNA research has confirmed that what we might term as modern humans did, in fact, interbreed with Neanderthal. In fact, it has been proven that a small fraction of the genomes of modern man contain Neanderthal remnants.

Neanderthal man came out of the same areas of Africa as did Homo Sapien about 400,000 years ago. The numbers of Neanderthals appear to have been somewhat limited, probably less than 100,000, most of which were concentrated in Asia and Western Europe. It was an invasion of this area by what we might term modern humans that both helped and damaged Neanderthal man.

Science long thought that it was the changing colder climate found in Asia and Western Europe that spelled doom for Neanderthal, but more recent research has shown that this was not true. In fact, the physical characteristics of Neanderthal appeared to be well adapted for these colder regions.[8]

Homo Sapien is thought to have developed about 200,000 years ago, also in West Africa and migrated in several waves into Western Europe where they interacted with Neanderthal about 100,000 years ago. Whatever happened is unknown, but it is believed that by 35,000 years ago, Neanderthal was basically extinct. For a long time, it was believed that Neanderthals and humans fought until there were no Neanderthal's left, but now it is accepted that this was not the case. What is now believed is that since Neanderthals and Humans engaged in sexual intercourse that the human may have inadvertently spread infectious diseases

---

[8] Geneticliteracyproject.org

to which human had developed some immunity but which, in the long run, were deadly to the Neanderthals[9].

Current research does show that it is conceivable that by the time of the human invasion their numbers were already low. It is theorized that about 70,000 years ago, there were perhaps 1,500 reproductive aged females among the Neanderthals. There is also the issue that the Neanderthals lived in small villages isolated form other villages. This led to a certain amount of inbreeding which in turn led to often recessive traits becoming more and more prevalent in the overall population which made the population as a whole more susceptible to diseases.

There was also the fact that their geographic isolation would have magnified this issue making it more difficult for natural selection to weed out bad mutations[10]. A more recent scientific analysis also found that the Neanderthal genome

---

[9] Ibid
[10] Study by John Hawks, Paleoanthropologist of the University of Wisconsin at Madison.

was comprised of genes that reduced their overall fitness by over 40% compared to Homo Sapiens.

It is theorized that the insertion of Homo Sapien DNA into that of Neanderthal may have actually extended the life of these Human cousins, but it was not a permanent solution. It should also be noted that such interbreeding programs are used today by the U.S. Fish and Wildlife Service to save dying species from extinction.

All of this having been said, it is clear that at one level, Homo Sapien conducted a somewhat positive intervention into the affairs of their Neanderthal cousins. But research does leave many questions unanswered. If there was research being conducted in West Africa by, let us say for the sake of argument, aliens to create a worker drone as suggested by Sitchin[11], was Neanderthal considered a dead

---

[11] Sitchin, Zecharia, The 12th Planet, Bear & Company, Rochester, Vt. And Toronto, Canada, 1976.

end in the development research and turned loose to sink or swim, as it were?

Clearly, if Neanderthals and Homo Sapiens could interbreed as is indicted by the DNA research, why were they so different in other ways? Compared to the birth rate of the Neanderthal, it appears that Homo Sapiens took after the proverbial bunny with a population explosion that literally overwhelmed others.

However, be that as it may, let us continue our examination of history to see if there is any other evidence of intervention by unknown forces with the affairs of the Human race.

CHAPTER TWO
UNEXPLAINED ADVANCES

Now notice, if you will, that the tools of both the Advanced Australopithecus and Neanderthal, a passage of more than 2,000,000 years were virtually identical, sharp stones. Additionally, physically, both species were thought to look alike, so frankly there seemed to be little in the way of improvements between the earlier Advanced Australopithecus and Neanderthal. So, for that extended period of time, there was little, if any, advancement in the affairs of man.

Then, like a bolt out of the blue, there appeared on the scene, about 35,000 years ago, a new model of man, Cro-Magnon. Here was a true Homo Sapien, defined as thinking man. Neanderthal was bigger and rougher than current humans, but scientists say that if you took a Cro-Magnon man and dressed him in a suit and tie, you could not pick him out of a crowd, he looked so much like us.

It was Cro-Magnon Man that did the unbelievably intricate and beautiful cave art that gave rise to the label of caveman. Cro-Magnon also made and wore clothes, made and used specialized tool and weapons. He lived in an organized clan that had a patriarchal hegemony. He also demonstrated the rudiments of a religion, worshipping the "Mother Goddess". He was also the first the bury his dead in something close to our religious ceremonies.

As research grew more sophisticated, it became clear that Cro-Magnon Man descended from a much earlier species of Homo Sapiens that lived in western Asia and North Africa about 250,000 before the appearance of Cro-Magnon Man.

The reader may wonder why this is important, but what it shows is that modern man apparently appeared only

700,000 after Homo Erectus and over 200,000 years before Neanderthal. This makes absolutely no sense what so ever.

What made this development even more baffling, according to Professor Theodosius Dobzhansky[12], was that this unusual development took place during a period when the Earth was enveloped in an ice age. At this point in the history of the planet, conditions for any type of major advancement were not favorable. He was also baffled by the fact that Homo Sapien lacks completely some of the peculiarities of the previously known types of species and has some that never appeared before. In other words, modern man was not the result of standard evolution.

There is also the question of why civilization developed when and as it did. According to most scholars, by all previous data, Mankind should still be without a

---

[12] Professor Theodosius Gryorovych Dobzhansky (January 25, 1900 – December 18, 1975) was a very well-known Ukrainian geneticist and evolutionary biologist. Much of his discussion of this topic came from his 1962 work entitled Mankind Evolving, Yale University Press, New Haven, Connecticut.

civilization. There are no obvious reasons we should be any more advanced than the tribes of the Amazon jungle[13].

Scientist try to avoid the obvious answer by pointing out that the primitive tribes live in isolation and that is the reason they are not more advanced. However, the question is what are they isolated from? On a larger scale, human civilization as a whole is isolated, but still advanced at a rapid pace.

Actually, as both Sitchin and Dobzhansky pointed out in their writings, the real puzzle is not why the primitive tribesmen are so backward, but why we are so advanced? It took mankind over 2,000,000 years to reach the stage of using tools, that is going from using a stone in its natural shape to modifying the stone to suit his purposes. By this reasoning it should have taken another million or so years to learn to use other materials to build structures. It is estimated

---

[13] Sitchin, Zecharia, The 12th Planet, Bear & Company, Rochester, Vt. And Toronto, Canada, 1976.

it should have taken early man 10,000,000 or so years to master mathematics, engineering and other scientific endeavors. But, amazingly, less than 50,000 years from Neanderthal Man, we are landing men on the moon. How is this possible?

Everything about Cro-Magnon man was new and frankly, revolutionary. Even his society was a marvel, from living in caves to traveling, building shelters, developing clothing, manufacturing tools, the development art and religion were all aspects of the civilization development by this species of man. It was as if Cro-Magnon had received training that Neanderthal and his predecessors did not.

Finally, though we cannot explain the appearance and sophistication of Cro-Magnon Man, we do know where he began his development of civilization, the Near East[14], very close to the area of the so-called Garden of Eden. Was

---

[14] His area of development were the uplands and mountain ranges that extend in a semiarc from the Zagros Mountains in the east through Ararat and Taurus ranges in the north, then down to the west and south to the hill lands of Syria, Lebanon and Israel.

Cro-Magnon Man created by the Gods as a newer model of servant?

WHERE DID EVERYONE GO?

As a side note, I should probably discuss one other discovery made in this semiarc of civilization. Though the mountainous region enclosed in this semiarc of civilization there are a number of caves. One of these caves was known as Shanidar. These caves have long been used as temporary shelter for herdsman tending their flocks or as homes for those fleeing danger.

In 1957, American archeologist Ralph Solecki[15] was excavating Shanidar when he stumbled upon the bodies of a family of 7 who had apparently taken shelter in Shanidar and been crushed by a cave in. From their remains he continued to excavate until he had removed all of the layers of debris.

---

[15] Ralph Stefan Solecki is an American archaeologist and a former member of the faculty at Columbia University. His best-known work were the excavations of the Neanderthal site at Shanidar cave in Iraq.

What he found was a clear record of Man's habitation in the area from 100,000 to approximately 13,000 years ago.

To his amazement, he discovered that culture showed not an advancement over the years but rather a regression or a less advanced standard of civilized life. From about 27,000 B.C. to approximately 11,000 BC the regression continued until it reached the point of an almost absence of habitation. In other words, man was almost completely absent from the area.

Then approximately 11,000 B.C. mankind reappeared, though this time it was Cro-Magnon man with an unbelievably higher cultural level that the previous inhabitants[16].

FROM A HUNTER TO A FARMER

For most of his history, man had been a hunter gatherer, clans and villages were mobile to follow the game

---

[16] Sitchin, Zecharia, The 12th Planet, Bear & Company, Rochester, Vt. And Toronto, Canada, 1976.

as it moved. Naturally, this lack of a dependable food source would tend to be a limit on the size of any clan or village so out of necessity, these roving bands were small, hence the necessity of inbreeding that we discussed earlier. However, when man returned to the Shanidar area around 11,000 B.C., he was no longer a roaming hunter/gather, something new had been added, he was now a farmer. Farmers are not mobile, but rather the bedrock upon which towns are built. So, of necessity man began to build houses and buildings, creating permanent settlements.

Normally, with anything new, such as a weapon or a new way of doing things, there is a period experimentation to see what works and what does not. However, in this instance, it appears that one day, mankind was hunting and gathering as his civilization was fading away and then suddenly they picked up the plow and started farming.

As Robert John Braidwood[17] and Bruce Howe wrote in *Prehistoric Investigations in Iraq Kurdistan*[18], genetic studies have concluded that agriculture began exactly where thinking man had built his first earlier, cruder civilization, in the Near East.

So, what changed an entire civilization virtually overnight. Perhaps it was an intervention by a higher power.

Though scientists rarely agree on anything, it is surprising that most scholars agree that the first farming venture of mankind was the cultivation of wheat and barley. While this is basically acceptable to most, the gradual, though continual process of domesticating and growing numerous other plants needed for human survival is surprising. In rapid succession, these domesticated plants

---

[17] R. J. Braidwood was born 29 July 1907 and died 15 January 2003. He was one of the founders of scientific archaeology and a leader in the field of Near Eastern history. It is believed that he was the basis for the fictional character of Abner Ravenwood from the Indiana Jones series.
[18] The Oriental Institute of the University of Chicago. Oi.uchicago,edu

included millet, rye and spelt, flax and a variety of fruit bearing shrubs and trees.

As Sitchin points out it appears that the Near East was a virtual genetic-botanical laboratory for the development of new food sources. For those who want to look to religion for the source of this guidance, it is in fact, surprisingly, the text of Genesis accurately describes the process of plant domestication.

It is also in keeping with tradition and with the Book of Genesis that shortly after man became a farmer, he became a shepherd. It should be remembered that according to Genesis, after Adam and his family were expelled from the Garden of Eden[19], Abel became a keeper of herd and Cain was a tiller of the soil.

---

[19] The Garden of Eden was located in the east, or to the east of Israel. It was in a land watered by four rivers of which two were the Tigris and the Euphrates. According to the Book of Genesis, the first orchard was in the highlands where these rivers originated in northeastern Mesopotamia.

Research has shown that scholars are correct that before man could become a herdsman, he had to become a farmer. Only through farming could larger communities grow which were required to allow the keeping of domesticated animals[20]. Dr. Zeuner felt that animal domestication was the result of socialization and not trying to change the environment in which men lived.

Mankind thrived with his cities and the new food sources that resulted. Then once again, something happened that added fuel to mankind's fire, in 7,500 B.C. he developed pottery. In other words, mankind developed art to a new level. It was the many uses that clay and pottery cold be put to that led to civilization leaving the airy abodes of the mountains and coming to the plains and the mud filled valleys.

By 5,000 B.C. the Near East was producing and exporting clay and pottery products that surpassed all others.

---

[20] Zeuner, Fredrick Everard, Domestication of Animals, Scientia, 1956

Then about 4,500 B.C. something happened and once again civilization stagnated. Excavations showed that the standard of life regressed and even the art produced was of a simpler design than previously. Once again stone utensils were present. Industrial sites that had specialized in producing clay products were abandoned[21]. Civilization was clearly dying.

Then out of nowhere, once again, rose a civilization beyond all imagining. Mankind was being given another chance. Civilizations do not spring forth fully developed, so from whence came this new energy to breathe new life into a dying civilization? Was this another intervention by a mysterious power?

---

[21] Melaart, James, Earliest Civilizations of the Neat East. 1965.

CHAPTER THREE
ANOTHER NEW BEGINNING

Clearly, based on the excavations at the cave of Shanidar, at one point in our history, the human race was dying out. In fact, for several thousand years what had been a frequent habitation, temporary though it might be, was virtually abandoned.

There was a very strong belief that our current civilization was a gift, so to speak, from Rome and Greece. However, even the Greeks reported that their civilization was merely a reflection of an earlier civilization that had its beginnings in Egypt.

The study of the prehistory of civilization received a shot in the arm through the efforts of Napoleon. When this military leader arrived in Egypt in 1799, he brought with him historians to study and explain to him he ancient monuments that doted he Egyptian desert. It was one of his officers that found the famed Rosetta Stone upon which was a proclamation written in 196 BC that was written in hieroglyphics as well as two other scripts. It was from this humble beginning that scholars went on to learn to read the ancient writings of Egypt which opened up to them the long history of this desert country.

Through diligent research from many sources, it was discovered that, in early times, there existed in Egypt a very high level of civilization that was traced back to at least 3,100 BC, over two thousand years before the marvels of Greece and Rome were even thought of by man. Though it was clear that Egyptian civilization was relatively ancient, it was not the very first vestiges of this third attempt at civilization.

Though such great Greek travelers such as Solon[22] went in search of the beginnings of civilization, he was quickly educated by the priests of Egypt. He was informed that civilization was much older than anyone could guess. Whether discussing the Minoans or the Mycenaean cultures, each one of the ancient cultures had a precursor. In final analysis, even the Egyptian priests agreed that beginnings of our civilization came from the Near East.

DORIANS

There also some other interesting facts that came to light. About the thirteenth century B.C. the Dorians[23] invaded Greece and about that same time period, after the Exodus, the Israelites invaded and took control of Canaan.

---

[22] Solon was an Athenian statesman, lawmaker and poet. Though most of his writings failed to survive the ages, he was written about by many of his fellow countrymen. During a visit to Egypt, described by Plato in his two dialogues entitled Timaeus and Critias, two Egyptian priests told him of the history of Atlantis.

[23] The Dorians were a Hellenic people speaking the Doric dialect of Greek, thought to have entered Greece from the north c. 1100 – 1200 BC. They settled in Peloponnesus and later colonized Sicily and southern Italy. Some believe that they originally came from the area of the Near East and were related to the Israelites.

There are those who believe that the Dorians and the Israelites are related in many ways, some have even suggested that they were both part of a larger tribe that broke up after the escape from Egypt.

It is true that the Dorians and Israelites had a lot in common. They were looking for a homeland and were extremely warlike. Against their forces the Greeks did not have a chance.

According to records left by the Greeks, over 3,000 years ago, the Dorians, a tribe of war-like people, swooped down from the north onto the Greek peninsula. The Dorians did not have a written language. They were not into art or music or literature. The Dorians were into war. The Dorians did not build cities. They destroyed them.

It was easy for the Dorians to conquer the many tribes who made their home on the Greek peninsula. Before Dorian rule, the villagers had stone weapons. They lived in small villages. They did not speak the same language. They did not work together. On the other hand, the Dorians were organized, well trained, and armed with far better weapons made of iron. It wasn't even a contest.

There are written records left by the ancient Greeks that tell how they moved their women and children from village to village, to try and save them from Dorian slaughter. They collected stones and made weapons in preparation for the next battle. But all written records soon stopped. The Dorians had taken over and written records were no longer the norm. For the next 400 years, the Dorians ruled. This period of time in ancient Greek history is called the Greek Dark Ages.

The various tribes on the Greek peninsula hated the Dorians, with good reason. The Dorians were cruel and brutal. But after 400 years of Dorian rule, it probably never occurred to the Dorians that the villagers might revolt.

Things started to change when a new profession rose on the Greek peninsula - that of storyteller. The storytellers were not Dorians. They were villagers, creative young men who traveled from village to village, telling stories of heroes, monsters and myths, and how people worked together to defeat a common foe. They told these stories with plenty of arm motions and body motions so that everyone understood the story, no matter what language they spoke. Soon, nearly all of the storytellers began telling their stories in the Greek language, to give their stories a common thread. It was a language the Dorians did not understand and did not bother to learn. The early Greek people *did* learn so they could better understand the stories. So, the Dorians allowed a conquered people to learn a common language that the Dorians did not understand. That was a big mistake. It allowed the villagers on the Greek peninsula, if they chose to do so, to talk of rebellion right under their noses.

Another really big Dorian mistake was to teach the villagers how to make iron weapons, weapons supposedly limited to Dorian use. It is thought that the Dorians tried to create a middle class of iron workers to make their weapons for them. However, they failed to realize that a sword does not know who is supposed to use it, it can be used by anyone.

It was actually thanks to the Dorians, that people all over the Greek peninsula learned to make and hide strong metal weapons. Because the Dorians allowed the traveling storytellers to speak freely in villages all over the peninsula, the early Greeks learned a common language, developed a common history, worshiped the same gods, believed in the same heroes, and were shown through the stories and myths they loved the many advantages of working together to defeat a common foe. Add to this the Dorians' insistence on rule by cruelty and oppression, and it was that the Dorians caused their own downfall.

Dorian rule came to an end when the Greeks banded together into city-states and kicked the Dorians out of Greece. Once free of oppression, these early Greek city-states might have chosen to establish a central government.

But the Greeks did not do that. Each Greek city-state remained an individual unit, with its own government and its own way of doing things. And the ancient Greek civilization was born, a civilization that went on to invent democracy, trial by jury, the alphabet, the Olympics, advances in architecture, literature, art, medicine, math and so much more. Welcome to ancient Greece!

ISRAELITES

The Israelites written of in the Bible went on to conquer Canaan, destroying the existing society in much the same fashion as did the Dorians in Greece. Professor Cyrus H. Gordon[24] believed that the Minoans on the Isle of Crete and the Israelites were related since an early Minoan Script known as Linear A was determined to be a Semitic language. He also found that the pattern of Minoan and Hebrew civilizations was fairly constant. Even looking the name of

---

[24] Gordon, Cyrus H., Forgotten Scripts: Evidence for the Minoan Language.

Crete, spelled Ke-re-ta by the Minoans was the same as the Hebrew word Ke-re-et which means walled city.

It is not our attempt to delve into cultural differences, but we discuss this to show that both the Dorians and Israelites moved their entire civilization based on the wishes of their gods. As for the cradle of civilization that appears to have existed in the Near East it is clear that the human race had sort of a reboot between the Neanderthal culture and Cro-Magnon as if the "new man" was modified to correct problems found in the "old man".

Just as the first two efforts at creating a civilization seemed to have their starts on the African continent, this third attempt had its beginnings in the Near East. So many of the underpinnings of our civilization had its start there that it is clear that if this was planned by some power, the Near East was where the actual work of creating a civilization took place.

For example, from this one area of the world came clear evidence that prior to the known civilizations were the Akkad and the Sumerian. Both achieved greatness in many areas. It was Sargon of Akkad that conquered the capital of Sumeria and took for himself both the title of "righteous ruler[25]" and the knowledge amassed by the greatest minds of that very early kingdom.

From the very early records discovered by archaeologists it was discovered that from Sumer came the knowledge of temple building, the working of gold and silver, the proper ways to plant gardens and the creation and use of bricks.

Another interesting commonality came to light after researchers read the records recovered from the desert sands. It seems that the gods took an active part in the building of their homes. Gudea, one of the best known of the rulers of

---

[25] It was discovered that the gods had to approve each ruler before he could take the throne.

INTERVENTION 43

Lagash, the Sumerian city conquered by Akkad was given detailed instructions of how to build the temples he boasted of in his writings. Moses built God a residence during the Hebrew travels through the desert. He built this residence based on detailed instructions he received form the one he called "Lord God". When King Solomon built the first temple in Jerusalem he did so based upon information he received in another set of detailed instructions. The instructions he received from God was the basis for his claim that the Lord had given him wisdom.

Still later when the prophet Ezekiel was involved in the building of the Second Temple, he said he was shown very detailed plans in a Godly vision by a person who had the appearance of bronze and who held in his hand a flaxen strong and a measuring rod.

Much earlier, Ur-Nammu, the ruler of the city of Ur said that his god ordered him to build a temple for the use of the god according to a set of detailed plans and gave him a measuring rod and a rolled string for his use in the laying out of the temple[26]. So, it would seem, if there was any truth to these oddly similar statements that their gods gave them instructions for the building of the temples, that they were dealing with very real entities who had very specific needs, not an ethereal being.

Turning once again to the ruler Gudea, he claims to have been given a plan for the building of the temple. In fact, one of his statues shows him seated with the tablet upon which this temple plan was engraved. In actuality, this simple floor plan he claims to have been given was the design of what became a seven-story ziggurat[27]. The successful completion of this project also revealed other important features about the civilization that produced these magnificent temples. Clearly, they had the organizational skill that involved creating architectural plans, the ability to

---

[26] Sitchin, Zecharia, The 12th Planet, Bear & Company, Rochester, Vt. And Toronto, Canada, 1976.
[27] Ibid

organize and feed a tremendous work force, prepare the ground for the building of this massive structure, to mold an untold number of bricks and prepare stones while bringing from afar rare metals and ores then work the ores and cast the metals to produce the decorations needed for the temple. Underpinning all of this would be the need to develop a form of writing with which to prepare the plans and specs for the building. Could all of this have come from a civilization in the third millennium B.C. without the help of an advanced civilization? I think not.

CHRISTIANITY

It may be hard for people today to understand but at one time, Christianity, now one of the major religions in the world was an outlawed cult. Caught worshiping could result in the death penalty. This all changed, literally overnight.

On October 28, in the year 312 AD, the army of the Roman Emperor Constantine I was advancing toward Rome to fight the army of Maxentius, another claimant to the throne. Records kept by scribes who traveled with Constantine, reported that shortly before the battle, a mysterious glowing object shaped like a cross appeared in the sky and hovered for some time over Constantine and his army.

Constantine came to believe that this was a sign and that it the sign of the cross was painted on all of their shields, that they would be victorious. He ordered that the sign of the cross be painted on every shield in the army. During the Battle of Milvian Bridge, Constantine's forces were victorious and he, not only became the sole ruler of the Roman Empire, but he also made Christianity the official religion of Rome[28].

---

[28] Maloney, Mack, UFOs in Wartime: What They Didn't Want You To Know, Berkley **Books, New York2011**

OTHER RELIGIONS AND OTHER MYSTERIOUS FIGURES

Additionally, also from religious teachings, this time from the Holy Bible, comes the story of Shadrach, Meshach and Abednego. On the orders of the ruler, these three unfortunates were thrown into a fiery furnace so that flames would consume them. However, when the King went to check on them, they were unharmed, sitting in the flames with a fourth individuals that mysteriously appeared inside the furnace and who was later identified as an Angel of the Lord[29].

The three early Christians were rescued by this mysterious stranger that no one saw walk into the guarded furnace. The actions of this mysterious figure two very interesting facts. One is that this Angel of the Lord, was able to become a physical being when necessary, as he was very clearly seen by the King who had ordered the three thrown

---

[29] King James Edition of the Holy Bible

into the furnace, and in doing so had the power to keep the flames at bay.

Now it is also interesting to note that for centuries, to even entertain this possibility, that Angels had a physical body when needed, was considered blasphemy by the Church[30]. To raise such questions regarding Angels becoming men and walking among us would quickly get the asker excommunicated by the religious elders.

Now the second possibility was that these three were rescued by a physical entity who had tremendous powers such that he could keep the flames at bay. So, did the gods come to rescue these three simply because they were believers? Not hardly. There was a very real political result of this daring rescue, the King gradually became a Christian based on his witnessing of this miracle[31].

---

[30] Prophet, Elizabeth Clare, Forbidden Mysteries of Enoch, Summit University Press, Livingston, MT, 1983.
[31] Remember that any science suitably advanced is indistinguishable from magic.

INTERVENTION

Then of course there was the incident involving John Wesley, the founder of the Methodist religion. As a result of his supposed blasphemy, an angry mob gathered to lynch him. He was said to have been saved by an Angel, though it was a very real appearing Angel. As a result of this intervention, not only was a life saved though the actions of this mysterious figure, but this fledgling religion gained a significant advantage and a large number of followers[32].

Even more interesting, and proof of a direct intervention on the part of some high power to save Western Civilization, is a story involving Attila the Hun.

In 439 AD the father of Attila and his brother died. The father had been a friend to Rome. Accordingly, Rome signed a treaty with Attila and his brother who were co-rulers of the Huns. However, claiming that Rome had breached the

---

[32] Ronner, John, Do You Have A Guardian Angel?, Mamre Press, Oxford, AL, 36203, 1985.

treaty, and after killing his brother so that he was the sole rule of the Huns, Attila invaded Italy in 452 AD[33].

The Romans were no match for Attila's death machine. The Huns swept the mighty Legions of Rome from the field each time they met until the Huns were camped a mere 20 miles from the gates of Rome itself. There was no doubt in anyone's mind that Attila would enter Rome and that would be the end of the Roman Empire. How different the world would have been if that had happened. Imagine if you will that even Christianity would have been reduced to the level of a cult rather than one of the main religions in the world and the religion of Attila the Hun would have been the dominate religion for a thousand years.

The Bishop of Rome, Pope Leo I, offered to go out and try to negotiate terms with Attila to save Rome. No one believed that he could do it, but the Emperor had nothing to

---

[33] There is also the story that the Emperor of Rome's sister Honoria had asked for Attila's help to get out of an arranged marriage with what she called a boring senator that her brother had selected. Attila decided that she would be his next bride and invaded Italy.

lose at this point and was willing to let him go on the off chance he might accomplish something.

So, it was that, on foot, Pope Leo I walked steadily toward the main camp of Attila, the terror of the east. He found the main cap at the confluence of the Mincio River and the Po River. The mighty Hun army was saddled and waiting for the word to advance when Pope Leo entered their camp and demanded to speak to Attila.

In a confrontation that could result in the changing of the world, Pope Leo ordered Attila, the man who had slaughtered millions in his long bloody career, the man who had only suffered one defeat on the battlefield in his entire career to turn back or face the wrath of St. Peter. To the shock of everyone, very probably Pope Leo I as well, Attila agreed and withdrew from, not only the environs of Rome but from Italy itself.

When asked by his servants why he had run from one doddering old man who literally spouted nonsense, Attila had responded that he had not fled from Leo but from the two fiery figures standing on either side of him waving swords. According to Attila, both of these figures, apparently seen only by him, informed Attila that unless he left Rome unmolested, they would kill him. So it was, that in religious parlance, two Angeles saved Rome and the early Christian church[34] not the military might of Rome.

It would appear obvious that the gods, for lack of a better term, want human kind divided rather than consolidated under one religion or one government. They also want to control what other religions teach to the masses. This is evidence that the current main religions were started by one or two individuals who had a vision in which they conversed with the "one true god" and then began to spread his word. Interesting if true.

---

[34] Ronner, John, Do You Have A Guardian Angel?, Mamre Press, Oxford, AL, 36203, 1985.

Now that we have seen some of the ways in which the human race as a whole was assisted in its survival, let us look at some of the more practical and visible ways "someone" intervened in the affairs of men.

CHAPTER FOUR

HOME OF THE GODS

Over the next few thousand years, the activities of the human cultures across the planet were reminiscent of the game of chess. There were wars, kingdoms were formed, and kingdoms were destroyed. Vast Empires were built up at the cost of much blood and death and then those vast empires were ground down into the dust from which it came. Each kingdom believed that by going to war they were following the orders of their gods. This is exactly like a vast board came with tokens being manipulated by unseen players. Or as the humans referred to them, the gods.

One country, especially, has been of fascination to those who believe that this planet has been visited by advanced alien species and that country is Egypt. Certainly, not the first successful civilization, Egypt has long been viewed as a sign that there was more going on that history has led us to believe.

Let us start with a review of the pyramids. These massive structures, there are several of which we are aware, would tax a modern building crew to erect, were said to be the nothing more than burial places of the Pharaohs. If this is correct, then the entire physical labor output of the entire country would be dedicated to creating a tomb for their ruler, who, in many cases, was a young vigorous man in the prime of life when he came to the throne. It doesn't make any sense that the entire workforce of the country would be dedicated to project that did nothing to benefit the country as a whole. If this is true, then how did Egypt come to be, at one point in history, the most powerful country in the known world?

History tells us that the massive stones used to build these edifices were moved and lifted using fallen trees as rollers and pulled by slaves with long ropes. What is interesting is that, according to archaeologist Richard Coslow, just one of the stones used in this construction was so massive that it would require ten men to lift 900 pounds each to move each stone. This was an impossible feat then as it is now. Even some of our most sophisticated construction equipment can't life some of the stones used to build the Great Pyramid. So how was it accomplished?

It should also be remembered that those in actual contact with the gods have reported very real physical features and needs expressed by these entities. For example, when the Hebrews wandered through the desert, Moses built a large tent for God's use. The instructions to Moses for its building required that the interior height be eight feet. Why would this be required unless the being planning to use this tent was 8 feet in height?

Additionally, that clan of the Hebrews that was to be the direct servants of Jehovah were required to sew bells into the hems of their robes so that they would not upon God unaware. How could someone sneak upon an omnipotent being? I do not claim that there is no God, but perhaps those who have played god over the eons are not what they claim.

CHAPTER FIVE
THE GODS ORGANIZE THEIR SERVANTS

It would appear that even among gods there are disagreements that can lead to war. However, in history in the case of gods, the actual fighting was done by their followers. In other words, humans.

Suppose, if you will, that there was a plan established by the gods of antiquity through which their human servants were to be ruled by a very well indoctrinated cadre of servants who were granted the title of King or Czar of Emperor. Ruling through their proxies, the gods could be assured that their wished would be carried out on Earth. Now suppose, if you will, that there was a second faction of gods who had a different plan that required that this ruling cadre be removed.

It is also interesting to note that in the case of most of the so-called civilized world, the rulers of the various countries all claimed to have the right to rule due to a special relationship with their god or gods. Even more interesting was the fact that the various ruling families, at least in Europe and some parts of Asia were related by blood and their lineages could be traced back for hundreds of years. So, is could be said that the wars between their countries were actually family squabbles and not attempts to destroy either country. No matter who won or lost the war, there was, in fact, a certain stability in our civilization. The winners got bragging rights and the losers simply went home and licked their wounds.

This special relationship between humans and their gods went back into pre-history. Zeus was said to disguise himself and pick out pretty human females for sex romps.

This led to the birth of Hercules and a number of other individuals who made a mark on history. Let us also not forget the Watchers spoken of in the Holy Bible who were said to have seen that the daughters of an were fair and took some of them as their wives. Their offspring, the Nephilim were said to be mighty men and it was also inferred that some of them may have been giants.

ALEXANDER THE GREAT

Many rulers claimed godly parentage that was used to account for their special status and their right to rule. Consider, if you will Alexander the Great[35] whose father was said to have been a god[36]. This was one of the reasons that his troops followed him across the known world, leaving hearth and home for years at a time. Additionally, it is said

---

[35] The man called Alexander the Great was actually King Alexander III of Macedon, a member of the Argead dynasty. He was born in Pella in 356 BC and succeeded his father Phillip II to the throne at the age of twenty. His mother claimed that she saw in a vision that his father was actually Zeus, the King of the Gods.

[36] Hart, Will, Ancient Alien Ancestors, Bear & Company, Rochester, VT. And Toronto, Canada.

that in all of his conquests he never lost a battle, a startling claim for a military leader.

It is interesting to note, however, that on at least two occasions, those piloting the UFOs took a direct hand in Alexander's affairs. During the 4th century B.C., Alexander set out to conquer the known world. This incident is said to have happened while Alexander's forces were attempting to force a river crossing under fire from their foes so that they could invade India.

Just as it seemed that Alexander's army would be successful, two silver shields, spitting fire from their rims descended from the clouds, and began to harass Alexander's forces until both the men as well as their horses and war elephants panicked and refused to go any further. Clearly, those who fly the UFOs had a plan that did not include Alexander conquering India. Frankly, these two silver shields that appeared out of nowhere is all that saved India from being subjugated by the mighty Alexander[37]. How different the world would be if India had been part of the Greek Empire.

The second incident took place in 332 B.C. during Alexander's conquest of the city of Tyre. This mighty walled city was located on an island just off the coast of present-day Lebanon. Tyre was controlled by the Persians and had incredibly thick walls and unusually designed defenses. The city was so strong that it had withstood Alexander's siege for months.

Finally, just when Alexander was contemplating giving up the idea of capturing Tyre, fie of the mysterious silver shields appeared in the sky over the city of Tyre. After making a number of revolutions around the city, one of the shields emitted a ray that caused a section of the mighty wall

---

[37] Maloney, Mack, UFOs in Wartime: What They Didn't Want You To Know, Berkley Books, New York 2011.

to collapse. Alexander's forces stormed through the breach and captured the city[38].

THE PLAN

All this ancient plan for stability established by the ancient ones, if that's what it was, began to change as a direct result of the participation of the United States. The founding fathers claimed that the United States was a unique experiment, the act of a free people. It has led to the creation of the most powerful country that the world has ever seen.

What was most interesting to me was that every one of the founding fathers was a member of a secret society and directly or indirectly a member of the elite. So, we must ask if the founding fathers came up with the idea of breaking away from England of their own free will or was the creation of a new political order part of a pre-ordained plan passed down to them from their secret society? It also boggles the mind that a rag tag army with few resources beat the most

---

[38] Ibid

powerful military machine in the world at that time to the point that they could sever all ties with their mother country? It makes no sense from either a logical or a military point of view.

For a student of history there is the question of how the Romanoff Family was removed from the throne of Russia. The Czar of all of the Russia's was an immensely powerful man backed by equally powerful nobles and the undisputed commander of a massive army. He was also related by blood to many other royal families throughout Europe who would not want he and his family murdered.

So how was it that a rag tag bunch of conspirators with little in the way of resources managed to, not only depose the Czar, but destroy the entire fabric of Russia Society and subvert the army that was sworn to protect the Czar with their very lives? It might come as a surprise to find out that the Russian Revolution was a success direct as a result of support from both the United States and Germany, who were supposedly enemies at the time.

Both Lenin and Trotsky received direct assistance from the U.S Government in both sneaking into Russia and raising the funds necessary to finance the revolution[39]. Note that this assistance was given to the Communist movement even though Russia was an ally in the fight against Germany. No wonder some foreign countries are hesitant to trust this country.

Lenin and Trotsky were given a large amount of gold bullion to finance their fight and this was transported to Russian on board a special train that was given clearance to cross Germany during a time of war. In fact, the German government actively, assisted U.S. agents in smuggling Lenin and his followers across Germany and into Russia to

---

[39] Allen, Gary and Larry Abraham, None Dare Call It Conspiracy, Double A Publications, Suite 403, 18000 Highway South, Seattle Washington 98188.

subvert the Russian government during a time of war. Consider the implication of this activity, if you will.

AN EGYPTIAN HOME

All of the above to the side, there is every appearance that the gods had their base of power in the Near East, in what might be referred to as the Eden Area[40] as we discussed earlier.

According to the writings of Zecharia Sitchin in the translation of the Sumerian tablets, the advanced being that came to the Earth, who he called the Annunaki, were the actual creators of the Human race. Humans were created by breeding Annunaki females with a pre-existing proto-human that existed on Earth. The result of this breeding program was to be a worker drone to mine resources from mines that still exist in Africa.

---

[40] The location of Eden was said to be at the confluence of four rivers, two of which were the Tigris and the Euphrates. Many researchers think that the Garden of Eden, assuming it existed at all, was located in this general area.

However, there was a falling out between the leader of the Earth expedition and his half-brother who was sent to take his place[41]. This rivalry eventually led to what was said to be a nuclear war. It is true that many researchers claim that the Sinai looks like a nuclear war took place there.

As a result of the forces unleased in this war, the gods had to leave their homes and seek shelter elsewhere. For this reason, many descriptions of the gods and goddesses of Greece and Rome bear a striking resemblance to those of the Middle east.

However, this is not all of the evidence that can be marshalled that Egypt may also have been a staging area for entities form another planet. As we move forward, we shall look at a number of other facts that support the proposition

---

[41] The original commander was Enki, the son of the King and his concubine. The half-brother replacement was the son of the King and his sister, making him full royal and senior to Enki though apparently younger in years. Note that in ancient Egypt, the Pharaoh was normally the son of the previous Pharaoh and his sister. Coincidence?

that ancient Egypt may have once served as a home of the Gods.

- The first sign of intervention by some power beyond that normally available to the ancient Egyptians were, of course, the pyramids. Even more unusual was the fact that the pyramids at Giza are positioned in a way that makes them a perfect match with the stars in Orion's belt. Two of the pyramids are the same height while the third on is half as high. In Orion's belt, two of the stars are equally bright while the third one is half as bright. The pyramids are also positioned in an almost perfect line with the North Magnetic Pole. This positioning of the pyramids would have required a massive working knowledge of science, geometry and astronomy. In fact, the knowledge needed to accomplish this monumental feat would have to be as advanced as we possess today.

- Among the many hieroglyphs left by the ancient Egyptians are some that have created a large amount of excitement among researchers. There are certain hieroglyphs that appear to show the ancient Egyptians using electricity. These hieroglyphs show people holding and using an electric lamp or a large light bulb. If this is true, how did these ancient people discover electricity so far back in time. It raises the question that perhaps the level of scientific achievement of the ancient Egyptians was much more advanced than we have previously believed[42].

- There are other hieroglyphs that raise even more questions. For example, consider if you will, these 3,000-year-old picture drawings that were found in the temple of Pharaoh Seti I in Abados, Egypt. These hieroglyphs show, very clearly, a helicopter, a plane,

---

[42] This also raises the question of the Baghdad Battery that was discovered by researchers in Iraq. This device was still capable of generating an electric charge after several thousand years.

and other futuristic looking flying machines. Before arguing that these interpretations are mistaken, anyone who has ever seen a helicopter will vouch that these drawing are very accurate representations of both a helicopter as well as a plane.

- Another item of proof that extraterrestrials made Egypt their home was found during the renovation of a house in Egypt. This proof consisted of some coins with the picture of the head and shoulders of an alien on one side and an alien spaceship on the other. It was no uncommon to put the head of an entity on a coin to commemorate some important.

- Then there was the unusual, perfectly preserved mummy found in a secret compartment in a small pyramid[43] near the pyramid of Senusret II. The structure of the skeleton looks nothing like the skeleton of a human. The face looks very different

---

[43] Said to be he burial place of the Queen to Senusret II.

form that of a human. Of even more interest, the body was surrounded by items that could not be identified by archaeologists. According to one source, the mummy, who served as an advisor to the Pharaoh was named Osirunet[44].

- Then there is the story of Akhenaten, a pharaoh who was said to be a major religious innovator and turned society on its head. After what has been called a "contact" in the desert, Akhenaten's view of the world changed. Upon his return form that meeting which he always refused to discuss, the began a program to covert Egypt from a polytheistic country to one that worshipped only one god, Aten or the Sun God. In fact, he even abandoned his capital and built a new city in the desert dedicated to the worship of Aten. It should also be noted that even the poetry of the time referred to Akhenaten being visited by

---

[44] The name means star or sent from heaven.

INTERVENTION 73

beings form the sky. Others claimed that Akhenaten was actually one of the sky beings. He single-handed destroyed the fabric of Egyptian society, which meant that he did not act alone but was apparently being guided.

- Then there is the famous Tulli Papyrus, which is said to be one of the best sources confirming an alien presence in ancient Egypt. This papyrus contains discussions of sightings of UFOs made during the reign of Pharaoh Thutmosis III. Though there are those who question the authenticity of this papyrus, it is still a major indicator that there were extraterrestrials in ancient Egypt.
- Then there is the fact that it has been reported that Egyptian hieroglyphs have been found on both the UFO that crashed at Roswell in 1947 and the one witnessed at Rendlesham Forest in 1980. Why would two UFOs over thirty years apart share

similar, if not identical ancient symbols? If it can be shown that these two symbols have a common denominator it would have major implications bout Egyptian society.

- Then finally, in the Egyptian home of Sir William Petrie, also known as Flinders Petrie[45], what were described as ancient artifacts were found hidden. One individual that examined them claimed that they were of unearthly origin. Among the items found were two mummified bodies that were allegedly that of extraterrestrials as well as items featuring symbols that could not be explained. The items were taken to Jerusalem's Rockefeller Museum and locked away.

Though there is little doubt, based upon the Sumerian tablets, that the original home of these visitors was in the area of Iraq, it does appear that after the happenings in the Sinai that the gods sought other homes. The evidence seems

---

[45] Flinders Petrie is considered one of the best Egyptologists in history.

fairly clear that one of these homes was in Egypt. Others of the gods appear to have migrated to Greece[46] and perhaps Rome. Are the gods of the near and middle east the same as on Mount Olympus and were they physical beings as opposed to ethereal gods? Surely, an ethereal god would not have to run from the results of a nuclear bomb as apparently took place here.

After this review, let us not forget the caution from the scriptures to not turn your back on a stranger because you may be turning away and Angel. This says to this author that, at least one school of thought, believes that Angels look like humans. So, with that in mind, let us look at more evidence that we may be looking at physical beings as opposed to what might be called gods.

---

[46] There is one story that Aphrodite swam across the Mediterranean Sea to establish a new home in Europe.

CHAPTER SIX
THE GODS GO TO WAR

After having to leave the Middle East which had been their home for thousands of years, and having gone to the trouble of establishing their new home in what they considered a hospitable place, such as Egypt, the question becomes what did they do next? It is evidence that these beings, no matter how powerful they may have been had many of the same failings as humans. They also had disagreement that eventually led to very destructive wars.

Most of our major religion tell us that the messengers of the gods, whether we are talking about a monotheistic single god, or a polytheistic group of gods, are Angeles. Angeles can be visible or invisible depending on the circumstances[47]. They also do not seem to be susceptible to the normal physical laws that we all have to obey, such as the ability of the Angel that rescued the three Christians from the fiery furnace we discussed in a previous chapter. Of course, this does make one wonder just what these messengers of the gods might be.

Not just Angels took it upon themselves to get involved in the wars of men. In regard to the Trojan War, it was Zeus himself, the King of the Gods who was said to have instigated this war in order to lighten the load on the planet Earth and reduce the number of men through war[48]. Then too, there were numerous stories of gods and demi-gods taking an active part in this struggle.

In very ancient times the patron of the Egyptian Army was known as Sobek, the Crocodile god. He was also

---

[47] There is a great deal of evidence that would lead us to believe that perhaps the concept of religion was taught to early man as a method of control. Certainly, every religion has a long list of does and don'ts. Certainly, a very certain way of controlling a massive population.
[48] Greek tale entitled Kypria.

known as the defender of the Egyptian people and the Pharaoh. This figure who had the head of a crocodile was said to have, at times, physically led the army. If he was a real figure, perhaps the crocodile head of a breathing device to allow him to survive in our atmosphere.

Sobek was said to be the son of Set, the god of war and hostility and Neith, the warrior goddess of hunting and warfare. There is much evidence that the entity known as Set was a physical being and ruled Egypt as Pharaoh Seti I. Of course, this is sheer speculation as the name Seti means of Set, so he may have been either consecrated to Set or descended form Set.

Then of course there was Osiris, brother of Set and an early king of Egypt. If Osiris was a physical being who ruled as king, then clearly Set was as well. Osiris was the husband of Isis, a well-known goddess of the Egyptian pantheon and mother of Horus who also ruled as King after defeating Set, the man who allegedly murdered and dismembered his father.

The Hittites ruled a vast area prior to the Trojan War. Their god was called TESHUB (translated as the Stormer) and in many battles the Hittites claimed that The Stormer took an active role smiting their enemies with his thunderbolts. The Hittites also worshipped the goddess ISHTAR and claimed to have seen her descend from the heaven to engage in combat with the enemies of the Hittites.

Even the Egyptians claimed that their god, Amon, appeared on the battlefield. In one specific battle, the Pharaoh, himself, Ramses II was cut off from his main forces by over 2,500 Hittite chariots. There was no way he could escape being captured or killed. However, according to Ramses II, Amon appeared on the battlefield and ordered the Pharaoh and his royal guard to charge against the amassed Hittite forces. According to the later inscriptions, the Hittite forces were enfeebled, unable to fire a single weapon against the Pharaoh[49].

There are also numerous stories about God, referring to the Hebrew Jehovah, using one country to punish another through invasion and conquest. Such is the case with Babylon conquering Israel or when God led his people into Canaan and ordered them to destroy the tribes already living there[50].

There is also the issue that the gods, or God, if you will, seemed to have an ego. If a people failed to obey his orders, he was not about having them conquered or destroyed. For example, consider if you will the fate of the northern kingdom of Israel as discussed in 2nd Kings 15:29 and 16:7-9. This Jewish kingdom was conquered and over 27,000 Jews were taken to Assyria as captives. Their crime in the eyes of their God – they failed to obey the voice of

---

[49] Sitchin, Zecharia, The Wars of Gods and Men, Bear and Company, Rochester, VT. And Toronto, Canada. 1990.
[50] Deuteronomy 20-16-17, King James Bible.

Jehovah their God. This does not sound like the actions of a benevolent God but rather the actions of a very human figure who wanted to punish those who failed to obey him.

That is not to say that there is no God, rather it looks at the primitive sate of the people of the Earth at that time and calls to mind the old saying that any science suitably advanced is indistinguishable from magic. Magic is normally performed by gods, and thus gods survive by having followers. These followers carry out the wishes of their gods, even if it sends them into battle.

If, as I believe, the guardians of civilization, as they seemed to have styled themselves, planned for the future of this planet and they take steps to protect that plan when their human subjects stray from the path called for in the plan. These guardians are either very long lived, which is stated in the religious doctrines of the times, or the descendants of the original planers who clearly adhere religiously to the plan.

Consider if you will an incident that took place during World War I. This war was considered the war to end all wars, though it began as another in a long line of family disputes. The Austrian Archduke Franz Ferdinand, nephew of Austrian Emperor Franz Joseph and heir to the throne of Austrian and Hungary, and his pregnant wife Sophia were assassinated by agents of the Black Hand[51] in Serbia which eventually led to World War I.

Prior to the assassination, most of the countries of Europe were ruled or controlled by an inter-related group of families from the same ancient bloodline. As a result, while there were wars previously, these were not planned as battles to the death. In fact, the rule of the three major powers in the game, England (Queen Victoria and then George V), Germany (Kaiser Wilhelm) and Russian (Czar Nicholas) were first cousins who knew each other very well. This began to change as countries formed alliances and jockeyed

---

[51] A secret military order.

for political advantage. The evidence is very clear that there was an unknown party working to overthrow the accepted order that had controlled civilization, at least in Europe for over a thousand years.

ANGELS AT WAR

Naturally, each side in this massive war had the firm belief that God was on their side. Additionally, at least in Europe, it was the same God. Religious leaders for both sides of this bloody conflict beat the war drums and promised that God would give them victory.

Many believe that only man goes to war, but there are even stories in the scriptures about Angeles going to war against each other, but that it for another book. Now I am going to give a couple of examples of Angles mixing it up in the wars of men.

THE ANGELS OF MONS

Some consider this story fiction while other swear by its truth. On August 22 and 23 in the year 1914, the first major engagement of the British Expeditionary Force occurred in the Battle of Mons. In this battle the Germans heavily outnumbered the British forces. There seemed little hope for the survival of the British forces against the much larger German forces.

On this battlefield was a company of British cavalry. Facing them was a much larger force of Germany cavalry[52] that was clearly readying itself for a final charge that would overwhelm the beleaguered British horsemen. Suddenly, the horses of the German force began to panic and then they scattered, running for the rear, totally out of control. Several of the German officers later claimed that the British force was joined by a host of figures astride white horses waving flaming swords[53]. Whatever may have been the truth of the matter, the British force escaped certain death and the German force was routed.

---

[52] Both sides used elite forces of cavalry to very great effect.
[53] Ronner, John, Do You Have A Guardian Angel?, Mamre Press, Oxford, AL, 36203, 1985.

If true this story would go a long way toward confirming that Angeles exist, however, this was not the only amazing story to come from that battlefield. The British Expeditionary Force was certainly not prepared for the might of the German Army. In another part of that sprawling engagement there was another British unit facing overwhelming odds.

This unit was surrounded and in readiness for what they perceived to be a final charge, they had fixed bayonets so that they could at least go down fighting. Just as the German forces began to move across the field toward them, the British noticed that they had been joined by reinforcements. However, these reinforcements were not what you might consider normal British soldiers as they were wearing chain mail and carrying long bows. These reinforcements consisted of line upon line of English long bowman.

Now certainly, this would seem to be a wild story but there were other witnesses present on that battlefield on that fateful day. German prisoners of war complained that the new comers could not be downed by rifle fire. Several German snipers who had been very successful in killing British officers in the battle were baffled when the leader of the bowmen seemed to completely ignore their very accurate sniper fire[54].

Then there are the biblical legends of the Angel Raphael coming to the aid of a man by the name of Tobias who wanted to marry a beautiful woman. This woman was a widow who had been married seven times before. Each of her previous husbands had been killed by a demon by the name of Asmodeus. Raphael assisted Tobias in defeating Asmodeus and he successfully married his betrothed[55].

---

[54] Ibid
[55] Ibid

These stories make it clear that ethereal or real, these beings, both Angeles and demons seem to be able to have a very real impact in the here and now. Clearly, there are forces far beyond our comprehension that control what happens on this planet. This knowledge is certainly in keeping with the teachings found in the Sumerian tablets regarding the Annunaki.

CHAPTER SEVEN
THE END OF THE OLD ORDER

For thousands of years, a few royal families from what was viewed as a Royal Bloodline ruled the major countries on this planet. However, what became known as World War I ended with the Germans on the losing end and several royal houses in complete disarray.

At the end of World War I the League of Nations came into being and there was hope for a lasting peace, which was not to be. Actually, rather than a force for peace, the League of Nations caused more strife than peace. There are many who believed that had the old order prevailed that Europe would have been a much more ordered place and World War II would not have happened, or not have happened when it did.

It is also interesting to note that at no time until President Wilson got involved in the peace process was there any intention to force the Royal families to give up their power. The original intent of the peace negotiations was for the royal families to remain in control as every recognized that this would result in much needed stability. It was at the urging of the British and United States participants that Kaiser Wilhelm was forced to abdicate. This power vacuum led directly to World War II.

President Wilson had proposed forming the League of Nations which was intended to be a one world government. It was only after it was revealed that there had not been any really "good guys" involved in the war that Wilson realized that he could never sell his plan for the one world government.

It also came to light in the aftermath of this devastating war that there had been other forces at work manipulating the human race into this war to end all wars.

This other force had orchestrated the manipulation of financial resources to force entire countries to dance to their tune. It also led to the creation of the Soviet Union. Was God, some other force, punishing a world that was not listening to his voice?

As if this international manipulation was not enough, average individuals were also being contacted by mysterious entities with messages of guidance. Strange things were seen crisscrossing the sky and occasionally the pilots of these sky craft would land to converse with the locals, not unlike the contacts discussed earlier when the Pharaoh Akhenaten was guided to change his entire society at the behest of the visitors from the sky.

As these contacts grew in number, the governments involved began to try and cover up the contacts, landings and crashes of these mysteries from the sky which shall be discussed in the next chapter. It seems that the trappings of these mysterious beings changed from the Biblical era where their observers were rather primitive to arriving in spaceships for the era where man had reached for the moon. Ate the Greys today's Angels? It would seem so.

CHAPTER EIGHT
STRANGE AIRSHIPS

Until the era of the Roswell crash, the contacts by more advanced beings seemed to be somewhat common and less awe inspiring even though more and more advanced technology was demonstrated by some alleged hidden source. For example, the Great Airship Mystery of 1897 is a case in point.

What became known as the Mystery airships or the phantom airships have been considered by many researchers to be a type of unidentified flying object, though the pilots appeared human as opposed to the more common Greys seen today. These mystery craft received world-wide publicity as a result of a series of newspaper reports that began in

California but soon spread across the country during late 1896 and early 1897.

According to a well-known UFO researcher, Jerome Clark[56], airship sightings were not confined just to the United States, but were actually being reported worldwide during the 1880s and 1890s. Typical airship reports involved night time sightings of unidentified lights, but more detailed accounts reported that some of these airships appeared to be comparable to what came to be known later on as a dirigible.

In addition to the normal reports of lights in the sky, there were also a number of reports of actual physical contact with those on board the craft. Reports regarding the crewmen and the pilots usually described them as human-looking, although sometimes the crew claimed to be from Mars or other exotic locales. In a number of cases, the pilots would

---

[56] Clark, Jerome, Unexplained, Visible Ink Press, 1998

give the witness money to run errands for parts that they claimed were needed for the craft.

It was popularly believed that the mystery airships were the product of some inventor or genius who was not ready to make knowledge of his creation public. For example, Thomas Edison was so widely speculated to be the mind behind the alleged airships that in 1897 he "was forced to issue a strongly worded statement" denying his responsibility.

It has been frequently argued that mystery airships are unlikely to represent test flights of real human-manufactured dirigibles as no record of successful sustained or long-range airship flights are known from the period and "it would have been impossible, not to mention irrational, to keep such a thing secret." However, there were in fact several functional airships manufactured before the 1896–97 reports but their demonstrated capabilities were no nearly as sophisticated as those shown by the mystery airships.

Most journalists of the period did not seem to take the airship reports very seriously, as after the major 1896-97 wave concluded, the subject quickly fell from public consciousness. The airship stories received further attention only after the 1896-97 newspaper reports were largely rediscovered in the mid 1960s and UFO investigators suggested the airships might represent earlier precursors to post-World War II UFO sightings.

The photo on the previous page depicted one of the Mystery airship as illustrated in the *San Francisco Call*, in November 1896

It is certainly interesting to note that the best-known of the mystery airship waves began in California in the year 1896. Afterwards, reports and accounts of similar airships came from other areas, generally moving eastward across the country. Some accounts during this wave of airship reports claim that occupants were visible on some airships, and frequent encounters with the pilots were reported as well. These occupants often appeared to be human, though their behavior, mannerisms and clothing were sometimes reported to be unusual.

Welsh Researcher Mike Dash probably described the situation best when he wrote the following about the 1896–1897 series of airship sightings:

Not only were [the mystery airships] bigger, faster and more robust than anything then produced by the aviators of the world; they seemed to be able to fly enormous distances, and some were equipped with giant wings.

The 1896–1897 airship wave is probably the best investigated of all historical anomalies. The files of almost 1,500 newspapers from across the United States have been combed for reports, an astonishing feat of research. The general conclusion of investigators was that a considerable number of the simpler sightings were misidentification of planets and stars, and a large number of the more complex the result of hoaxes and practical jokes. A small residuum remains perplexing.

THE BEGINNING

Research has shown that The *Sacramento Bee* and the *San Francisco Call* reported the first sightings of the Mysterious Airships on November 18, 1896. Witnesses reported a light moving slowly over Sacramento on the evening of November 17 at an estimated 1,000-foot elevation. Some witnesses said they could see a dark shape behind the light.

A witness named R.L. Lowery reported that he heard a voice from the craft issuing commands to increase elevation in order to avoid hitting a church steeple. Lowery added that he believed the apparent captain to be referring to the tower of a local brewery, as there were no churches nearby. Lowery further described the craft as being powered by two men exerting themselves on bicycle pedals. Above the pedaling men seemed to be a passenger compartment, which lay under the main body of the dirigible. A light was mounted on the front end of the airship. Some witnesses reported the sound of singing as the craft passed overhead.

The November 19, 1896, edition of the Stockton, California, *Daily Mail* featured one of the earliest accounts of an alleged alien craft sighting. Colonel H.G. Shaw claimed that while driving his buggy through the countryside near Stockton, he came across what appeared to be a landed spacecraft. Shaw described it as having a metallic surface which was completely featureless apart from a rudder and pointed ends. He estimated a diameter of 25 feet and said the vessel was around 150 feet in total length.

Three slender, 7-foot-tall (2.1 m), apparent extraterrestrials were said to approach from the craft while "emitting a strange warbling noise." The beings reportedly examined Shaw's buggy and then tried to physically force him to accompany them back to the airship. The aliens were said to give up after realizing they lacked the physical strength to force Shaw aboard. They supposedly fled back to their ship, which lifted off the ground and sped out of sight.

Shaw believed that the beings were Martians sent to kidnap an earthling for unknowable but potentially nefarious purposes. This has been seen by some as an early attempt at alien abduction; it is appears to be the first published account of explicitly extraterrestrial beings attempting to kidnap humans and attempt to get them into their spacecraft.

- The mystery light reappeared over Sacramento on the evening of November 21. Reports show that this craft was also seen over the cities of Folsom, San Francisco, Oakland, Modesto, Manteca, and

Sebastopol in California's wine country as well as several other cities later that same evening and was reportedly viewed by hundreds of witnesses.

- One witness from Arkansas – allegedly a former state senator by the name of Harris claimed that he was told by an airship pilot (during the tensions leading up to the Spanish–American War) that the craft was bound for Cuba, to use its "Hotchkiss gun" to "kill Spaniards".

- In one account from Texas, three men reported an encounter with an airship and with "five peculiarly dressed men" on board who asserted that they were descendants of the lost tribes of Israel, and had learned English from the 1553 North Pole expedition led by Hugh Willoughby.

- On February 2, 1897, the *Omaha Bee* reported an airship sighting over Hastings, Nebraska, the previous day.

- An article in the *Albion Weekly News* reported that two witnesses saw an airship crash just inches from where they were standing. The airship suddenly disappeared, with a man standing where the vessel had been. The airship pilot showed the men a small device that supposedly enabled him to shrink the airship small enough to store the vessel in his pocket.

- On April 10, 1897, the *St. Louis Post-Dispatch* published a story reporting that one W.H. Hopkins encountered a grounded airship about 20 feet in length and 8 feet in diameter near the outskirts of Springfield, Missouri. The vehicle was apparently propelled by three large propellers and crewed by a beautiful, nude woman and a bearded man, also nude. Hopkins attempted with some difficulty to communicate with the crew in order to ascertain their origins. Eventually they understood what Hopkins was asking of them and they both pointed to the sky and "uttered something that sounded like the word *Mars*."

- An April 16, 1897, a story published by the *Table Rock Argus* claimed that a group of "anonymous but reliable" witnesses had seen an airship sailing overhead. The craft had many passengers. The witnesses claimed that among these passengers was a woman tied to a chair, a woman attending her, and a man with a pistol guarding their apparent prisoner. Before the witnesses thought to contact the authorities, the airship was already gone.

- An account from Aurora, Texas, related in the Dallas Morning News on April 19, 1897, reported that a couple of days before, an airship had smashed into a windmill – later determined to be a sump pump – belonging to a Judge Proctor, then crashed. The occupant was dead and mangled, but the story reported that the presumed pilot was clearly "not an inhabitant of this world." Strange "hieroglyphic" figures were seen on the wreckage, which resembled "a mixture of aluminum and silver ... it must have weighed several tons." In the 20th century, unusual metallic material recovered from the presumed crash site was shown to contain a percentage of aluminum and iron admixed.[citation needed] The story ended by noting that the pilot was given a "Christian burial" in the town cemetery. In 1973, MUFON investigators discovered the alleged stone marker used in this burial. Their metal detectors indicated a quantity of foreign material might remain buried there. However, they were not permitted to exhume, and when they returned several years later, the headstone – and whatever metallic material had lain beneath it – was gone.

- An account by Alexander Hamilton of Leroy, Kansas, supposedly occurred around April 19, 1897, and was published in the *Yates Center Farmer's Advocate* of April 23. Hamilton, his son and a tenant witnessed an airship hovering over his cattle pen. Upon closer examination, the witnesses realized that a red "cable" from the airship had lassoed a heifer, but it had become entangled in the pen's fence. After trying unsuccessfully to free the heifer, Hamilton cut loose a portion of the fence, then "stood in amazement to see the ship, cow and all rise slowly and sail off." Some have suggested this was the earliest report of cattle mutilation.

Among the many sources available that discuss the 1897 Airship Mystery, one of the best is by author Michael Busby. There is quite a bit of information available that cannot be presented here. Of course, the 1897 mystery was not the only unusual things that happened prior to World War I. There were also stories that surfaced that there were sightings prior to 1896/97.

In 1868, writer Charles Fort cited a mystery airship sighting over the town of Copiapo, Chile. It was described as a gigantic, shining bird that driven by a noisy motor[57]. This description would seem to be a precursor to the shiny craft talked of in the 1940s.

In a variation of the usual airship, on July 29, 1880 two witnesses in Louisville, Kentucky saw a flying object described as "a man surrounded by machinery which he seemed to be working with his hands" with wings protruding from his back.

Merely a month later, a similar sighting happened in New Jersey. It was written at the New York Times that "it was apparently a man with bat's wings and improved frog's legs... the monster waved his wings in answer to the whistle of a locomotive."

---

[57] Fort, Charles, The Book of the Damned, Boni and Liveright, 1919

In 1887, there was another wave of sightings of these mystery airships that has not received much in the way of publicity. This time the sightings were primarily on the east coast of the United States.

THE INCIDENTS OF 1909

So that the reader can understand that the airships seen in 1897 were not the only unusual things sighted in the sky, there was a series of mystery airship sightings in 1909 in the New England are of the United States, New Zealand and various European locations. A number of later reports surfaced from the United Kingdom for the years 1912 and 1913.

However, by this time the mystery airships did not raise as much excitement as previously. After all, by 1913 airship technology was well advanced[58] making the prospect that these may have been small, private airships rather than

---

[58] Count Ferdinand von Zeppelin had been flying his massive airships and even carrying passengers and freight for almost ten years by this time.

evidence of extraterrestrial visitation or newspaper hoaxes more reasonable.

Wallace Tillinghast, a Massachusetts businessman, gained notoriety for claims he was responsible for the 1909 wave due to an airship he had built, but his claims were never substantiated. In fact, it was never proven who was responsible for any of these airship sightings.

There is another contender for the title of mystery airship investor. As discussed by Dennis G. Crenshaw[59] in his interesting book, Charles A.A Dellschau purportedly documented the creation of these unique craft by the Sonora Aero Club. According to the writing left to the world by Dellschau when he died in 1923, the crafts were created using an anti-gravity gas invented by one of the club members. According to Dellschau, they turned over a series

---

[59] Crenshaw, Dennis G. and Pete Navarro, The Secrets of Dellschau, Anomalist Books, 2009.

of experimental aircraft over 50 years before the Wright Brothers got off the ground.

<u>AND SO</u>

So, whoever may have been the inventor of these mystery airships, there is no question that until 1903, these airships were the most advanced aerial vehicles on the planet and were seen in almost every country in the world. Were our keepers using their prowess to keep an eye on our development as a culture? This certainly seems to be a very strong possibility.

CHAPTER NINE
MYSTERIOUS AERIAL ATTACKS

As human technology has advanced, it seems that the technology demonstrated by what we call UFOs has also advanced. There has also been a very clear interest demonstrated by those who use the UFOs to determine the state of human military preparedness as we shall see. This has especially been true during times of war as if these onlookers are trying to determine what advances we have made in our military might.

WORLD I

We have spoken earlier about the appearance of what many call Angels on the battlefield to influence the outcome of various campaigns or battles, but this is what might be viewed as an isolated event of direct involvement to change the outcome, not a dispassionate watching to determine the state of military readiness.

There are a number of encounters that took place during World War I between human warriors and those who in earlier times were looked at as veritable gods. For example, even someone as experienced in the air as Captain Eddie Rickenbacker was very clear when he stated that *UFOs are real. Too many good men who do not experience hallucinations have seen them*[60].

Wartime experiences with UFOs were not limited to the Allied Forces, however. Even someone as experienced as Baron Manfred von Richthofen[61] has interactions with these mysterious watchers. On March 13, 1917, the Red Baron and his wingman Peter Waitzrik[62] took off from their base in Belgium. An hour into their mission, the two came

---

[60] In Mattweb "Military UFO Quotes," UFO Evidence: Scientific Study of the UFO Phenomenon and Search for Extraterrestrial Life.
[61] The famous Red Baron.
[62] Peter Waitzrik spent his long career as a Captain for Lufthansa where he was forbidden from discussing what he had seen.

upon a large metallic disk ringed by undulating orange lights.

According to Peter Waitzrik, the metallic dish was about 136 feet in diameter compared to the 28 foot, ten and one quarter inch wingspan of their own craft. Upon sighting the disk, The Red Baron immediately attacked the mysterious craft firing 7.92-millimeter rounds from a single Spandau machine gun and the disk immediately crashed into the woods. As the Baron and his wingman circled the crash site, they saw two little baldheaded guys climb out of the wreckage and run away.

When the two fliers returned to their airfield and reported what they had seen, both were ordered to never mention what had happened and what they had seen to anyone, ever. The Red Baron died during the war and Peter Waitzrik never discussed the incident until after he retired as a pilot in 1999[63]. As far as German Air Force records are concerned the incident never happened. However, this is in keeping with the habits of almost every military in the world. The presence of UFOs on the battlefield must be kept secret.

On April 14, 1917, one week after Congress declared war on Germany, three members of Company L of the 6th Massachusetts National Guard were guarding the Portsmouth Naval Shipyard in Maine[64]. Portsmouth had long been considered a very strategic military target and as such during time of war was heavily guarded.

Normally, this would be considered something of a boring assignment, but not on this night. It was about 2:30 am on the morning of April 14 with these three sentries

---

[63] Berger, Joe, "German Fighter Ace Red Baron Shot Down a UFO in 1917., Weekly World News, August 31, 1999.
[64] Hall, Michael D., UFOs: A Century of Sightings, Galde, Lakeville, MN, 1999.

spotted an aerial vehicle flying at a very slow speed directly toward their location[65].

As reported later, what really puzzled the National Guard soldiers was that the aircraft they spotted was completely silent, unlike the very loud aircraft of the times that they were somewhat familiar with. As the craft got closer, it made as if to dive toward the bridge upon which the three soldiers were stationed. In compliance with their orders to let no one or nothing enter the Naval Yard without authorization, the three soldiers began to fire at the unknown craft. Their primary weapon was the M1903 Springfield Rifle, which frankly should not have had any effect on the craft. However, in response to the fire from the sentries, the craft took off at a terrific speed, still making absolutely no detectable sounds whatsoever.

---

[65] Joseph, Frank, Military Encounters with Extraterrestrials: The Real War of the Worlds, Bear and Company, Rochester, VT. And Toronto, Canada.

As has been seen in regard to each report of UFO involvement, the military has always responded with a high-level investigation and this incident was no exception. The commanders of the Massachusetts National Guard, in conjunction with the military conducted several investigations of this incident.

The Massachusetts National Guard determined that neither civilian nor military craft, neither American or foreign had been involved in the incident. In fact, at the time there were only a few civilian pilots in the entire state and none of them could have flown after dark nor done the activities described by the sentries. Additionally, based on the speed demonstrated by the unknown craft reported, there was no way that the craft could have been a German aircraft or frankly produced by any country on the planet.

Naturally, the initial supposition by higher headquarters was that the sentries had merely imagined they saw an airplane and they were in for a lot of grief from both their peers as well as their superiors. However, over the next few days a number of additional both military and civilian eyewitnesses reported similar aircraft in the immediately vicinity of the shipyard. In fact, one witness reported that the aircraft that he saw sported a pair of green lights which was not something carried by aircraft until the 1920s[66].

The final conclusion of the numerous investigations that took place into this incident was that while no one could ever determine specifically what, or who, was flying over one of the most sensitive naval installations in the country, there was no doubt that the incident happened.

UFOS ON THE ATTACK

Perhaps it was fortunate that the sentries at the Portsmouth Naval Shipyard were a little trigger happy. Though it has not been widely reported in the UFO literature, there were a number of incidents where these mysterious aircraft went on the attack against ground installations.

---

[66] Ibid

Records indicate that prior to the incident at Portsmouth Naval Yard, there was a mysterious bombardment of other targets by mystery aircraft. As might be suspected, this was a military target, though privately owned by the DuPont Company.

This bombardment took place on January 10, 1916, approximately 15 months before the fly over of the Portsmouth Naval Yard[67]. This target was located at the DuPont gunpowder factory located at Carneys Point, New Jersey. The destruction was centered around a glazing house, which was a facility for sealing explosives in travel protected glass containers. Carneys Point was a very important munitions factory that had expanded its production facilities to meet the anticipated needs of the American military for the war everyone knew was coming.

On January 11, 1916, only nine miles away across the Delaware River, another Dupont facility that

---

[67] Ibid

manufactured munitions, called Hagley's Yard, had several of its powder mills destroyed by two massive explosions. Within the net twenty-four hours, a third massive explosion destroyed another powder mill[68].

January 14, 1916, an acid house at DuPont's Gibbstown, New Jersey plant blew up. Two weeks after this, five buildings at the Carney's Point plant burned to the ground. On February 4, 1916, a tremendous fire broke out in a photographic studio at the Carneys Point facility.

On February 6, 1916, the munition works at DuPont's Tacoma, Washington plant exploded without warning. Then as if this was not enough, beginning on the night of February 14, 1916 during a time of year not known for many fires, being in the dead of winter, over a period of just sixteen hours, no less than 39 mysterious fires broke out all across the city of Philadelphia.

---

[68] Ibid

On February 15, 1916, the Gibbstown factory was again ravaged by unexplained fires. On February 17 and then again on February 24 the Carneys Point facility was severely damaged by two unexplainable fires. As icing on the cake, one might observe, DuPont's Deep-Water Point station from which most of their explosives were shipped literally blew off the map on February 22, 1916.

Of course, the natural suspicion would be to blame saboteurs for the death and destruction, but in 1916, the United States was not at war with Germany and the German government was doing everything it could to keep the U.S. out of the war. Most of the explosives destroyed were earmarked for shipment to allied forces, but to attack the United States in such a fashion would have been resulted in a declaration of war against Germany, or whoever was responsible for the explosions and the fires.

Other suggestions have point to poor management on the part of the DuPont company, however, for the previous nine years there had not been a single mishap at any of the many DuPont facilities and even the explosion in 1907 had been a minor one limited to a single building. However, in 1916, the destruction was at four different factories in three different states[69].

However, what has rarely been mentioned and certainly not thoroughly investigated were the reported sightings of aerial craft flying over the various facilities during a period of time when there were no known planes in the area, civilian or military. Witnesses reported a mystery plane above downtown Wilmington, Delaware, hovering around the DuPont offices and a railroad worker reported over the power plant shortly after the Hagley Yard explosion.

On January 31, 1916 a strange aircraft was seen circling silently over the Gibbstown plant shortly after the

---

[69] Ibid

plant exploded. Then witnesses[70] reported that a white light appeared suddenly over the Deep-Water Point Section of the plant that was later destroyed.

On February 17, 1916, a lookout manning the fire tower at Ellis, outside Ashland, Wisconsin reported a large bright light that flew low around the Barksdale DuPont plant[71]. The plant was of particular importance to the U.S> Military as it produced not only dynamite but the much more powerful triton[72] explosive.

A review of witness reports reveals that the sightings of these mystery aircraft were concentrated around industrial and military locations across the region. In fact, during the period of these mystery explosions and fires, literally

---

[70] One witness was a former Marine and head of DuPont's Security Police at the Carneys Point facility.

[71] This particular plant was the largest munitions manufacturer in the state and employed over 2,300 hundred employees.

[72] An explosive consisting of a yellow crystalline compound that is a flammable toxic derivative of toluene and much more powerful than dynamite.

thousands of unknown aircraft reports were turned in to authorities[73].

It should also be mentioned that these mystery aircraft not only paid special attention to the DuPont facilities we have discussed, but also on other factories across the country that produced war supplies for our military and also for export to the allies. Other examples of this area spying consisted of craft over the rifle manufacturing plant in Eddystone, New Jersey and the DuPont gunpowder yard at Coatesville, Pennsylvania.

One last example of another mystery explosion took pace in July 13, 1916 took place at the Black Tom facility, New Jersey's major munitions depot. Just before the tremendous explosion, that registered 5.5 on the Richter Scale, witnesses reported seeing a strange looking silver airplane

---

[73] Watson, Nigel, UFOs of the First World War, History Press.

The *Philadelphia Enquirer* from February 13, 1916 reported that a "foreign war contrivances" was seen suspended directly over the Italian freighter Bologna as she was taking on a cargo of explosives at the Deep-Water Point. Additionally, there were reports that mystery aircraft were seen flying low over and seeming to probe the Ingersoll-Rand, Edison Cement and Taylor Wharton companies in New Jersey.

It should also be kept in mind that the interference with war production seen in 1916 was not an isolated event. Evidence has shown, and we will discuss, similar incidents that have continually happened and continue to happen even today.

It is also interesting to note that senior members of our government were not totally unaware that all of these explosions and fires might be part of a plan to interdict our ability to defend ourselves. There was document that reported that John Dewey, of the Carnegie Endowment for

International Peace, who was well known as a philosopher, psychologist and educational reformer was addressing a visiting Japanese delegation in 1917. His opening statement was quite revealing. He said *"The best way to cause all the people of the world to come together in one world government and end war forever would be if we were attacked by some other species from some other planet.*[74]*"*

It would appear that those highly placed knew or suspected that we were dealing with an alien species that did not want us to upset the existing order of things by working with the allies to defeat the Germans.

The evidence is certainly circumstantial and would not stand up in any court of law, but it is clear that some unknown power, demonstrating abilities and technology far beyond that of any country on earth at the time went out of its way to try and interfere with the production of war

---

[74] This was very similar to a statement made by President Ronald Reagan.

materials that would later be used to upset the accepted order of things in Europe.

A MYSTERIOUS BLIMP ATTACK

By the end of the Great War, as it was called, the use of blimps by the Germans to attack England was old news[75]. However, on the night in question January 31, 1916, the unusual air craft floating above the England Capitol was not the normal German blimp that British Royal Naval Air Service sub-lieutenant J. E, Morgan expected to encounter. However, he was game to take it on.

This encounter was discussed in detail in a book written by, then Captain, J. E. Morgan in 1925 entitled *German Air Raids on Great Britain, 1914-1918*. He described the craft he encountered as having a row of lighted windows and looking something like a railway car.

---

[75] The very first blimp attack on London was in 1915, but it was not a common occurrence until later in the war.

Having no machine gun mounted on his plane, he fired at the craft with his service pistol. Immediately, it took off at a very high rate of speed straight up. It went so fast that Morgan began to believe that his own plane was descending and eventually, becoming disoriented, he wound up crashing into a marsh.

No one accused him of imagining the incident as other witnesses, to include another pilot, also saw a very bizarre craft n the skies over London. However, Morgan did achieve one distinction, he became to first person to shoot at a UFO from the air.

CHAPTER TEN
AN EARTH-SHATTERING KNOWLEDGE

It seems clear that there was a third power, or maybe a fourth power, taking part in World War I. It also seems very clear that our government knew, or least suspected that this was the case and looked for ways to deal with this unexpected problem. It also explains how we were able to develop weapons needed to defend ourselves in the 1930s as we shall see in this chapter.

Author Paul Blake Smith published a formerly classified memo written by Franklin D. Roosevelt in his book entitled MO41: The Bombshell Before Roswell[76]. This memo was classified as Top Secret when it was written on

---

[76] Smith, Paul Blake, MO41: The Bombshell Before Roswell, W & B Publishers, St. Louis, MO, 2016

February 22, 1944. It was on White House stationary read as follows: *"The special committee on non-terrestrial science and technology is coming to grips with the reality that out planet is not the only one harboring intelligent life."*

There has been much discussion over the years about what has become known as the Battle of Los Angeles which took place on February 25, 1942. In this incident, numerous military units stationed in and around Los Angeles fired upon what they believed was an approaching aerial fleet of Japanese aircraft. None of these craft returned fire or even took any steps to evade the wave of munitions fired at them. As far as anyone knew, these mystery aircraft just flew off into the sky never to be seen again.

As with most UFO related events, the initial story is not exactly the true story. In fact, the aerial force flying over Los Angeles did have casualties. Since Washington DC leaks like a sieve, it is not surprising that classified memoranda regard an incident of this magnitude would be leaked.

In this instance there was a classified memo sent from President Franklin D. Roosevelt to General Georgia C. Marshall dated February 27, 1942. According to the text of this leaked memo, President Roosevelt was concerned about the materials recovered in a previous crash. The memo read as follows:

"I have considered the disposition of the material in possession of the Army that may be of great significance toward the development of a super weapon of war. I disagree with the argument that such information should be shared with our ally the Soviet Union[77]*. Consultation with Dr. Bush and other scientists on the issue of finding practical uses for the atomic secrets learned from the study of celestial devices precludes any further discussion and I therefore authorize Dr. Bush to proceed with the project without further delay. The information is vital to the nation's superiority and must*

---

[77] Several of FDR's close friends and associates during his time as President were later revealed to be either Communist sympathizers or secretly working for the Soviet Union. So, it is not surprising that he would be urged to turn such advanced equipment over to the Soviets

remain within the confines of state secrets. Any further discussion on the matter will be restricted to General Donovan, Dr. Bush, the Secretary of War and yourself. The challenge our nation faces is daunting and perilous in this undertaking and I have committed the resources of the government towards that end. You have my assurances that when circumstances are favorable and we are victorious, the Army will have the fruits of research in exploring further applications of this new wonder."

FDR[78]

Then there was another leaked Memo from General Georgia C. Marshall to President Roosevelt dated March 5, 1942 that contained some very interesting references to the recovery of craft form the Battle of Los Angeles. This leaked memo states:

"Regarding the air raid over Los Angeles it was learned by Army G2 that Rear Admiral Anderson has informed the War Department of a naval recovery of an unidentified airplane off the coast of California with no bearing on conventional explanation. Further it has been

---

[78] Holcomb, Larry, The Presidents and UFOS, St. Martin's Press, New York, 2015.

revealed that the Army Air Corps as also recovered a similar craft in the San Bernardino Mountains east of Los Angeles which cannot be identified as conventional aircraft. This Headquarters has come to the determination that these mystery airplanes are in fact not earthly and according to secret intelligent sources they are in all probability of interplanetary origin. As a consequence I have issued orders to Army G2 that a special intelligence unit be created to further investigate the phenomenon and report any significant connection between recent incidents and those collected by the director of the office of Coordinator of information,

G.C. Marshall[79]

Those who have investigated these documents have determined that they have a high level of authenticity. If true, it clearly shows that the President of the United States and the U.S. military knew that there was an extraterrestrial presence on this planet as early as the spring of 1941 and there is evidence that they knew of this presence even earlier. One thing is certain based on these two memos, FDR was

---

[79] Ibid

not aware of the recovery of the two craft relating to the air raid on Los Angeles at the time he wrote his February memo, so there were earlier recoveries of craft by U.S. military forces that had previously been kept secret from the American public.

The issue regarding these mystery craft was apparently considered above Top Secret with only a few people being in the loop, so to speak. Additionally, the fact that these mystery craft were acting with hostile intent, as was clearly the case during World War I, was something that none of the governments of the world wanted to get out to the public. This set the background for the creation of what has become known as Operation Majestic 12 by President Truman.

There was another memo referencing this mysterious program written by President Truman, and stamped top secret eyes only, and sent to Secretary of Defense James Vincent Forrestal. In this memo, President Truman wrote:

Dear Secretary Forrestal:

As per our recent conversation om this matter, you are hereby authorized to proceed with all due caution upon your undertaking. Hereafter this matter shall only be referred to as Operation Majestic Twelve.

It continues to be my opinion that any future considerations relative to the ultimate disposition of this matter should rest solely with the Office of the President following appropriate discussions with you, Dr. Bush and the Director of Central Intelligence. (See Appendix A[80]).

It is clear that President Truman wanted to keep a hand on position in regard to the flying saucers that were causing such chaos and confusion in certain areas. Even Truman's Air Force aide, General Robert Landry spoke of the President's great interest in flying saucers. He discussed this at some length in an oral history he did for Columbia University. He did make it clear that Truman wanted to be updated every three months by the Central Intelligence

---

[80] Ibid

Agency regarding any new information available regarding the flying saucer matter.

Under Truman's administration, the military went to great lengths to cover up information relative to the very existence of flying saucers. A prime example of this is the situation that developed regarding UFO crashes at Corona and Roswell, New Mexico.

ROSWELL – THE REST OF THE STORY

In the telling and retelling of the story of the UFO crash at Roswell, a few important facts were obscured from civilian researchers by the military. General Roger Ramey, the commander of the Eighth Air Force went to great lengths to make out Colonel Blanchard, the commander of the 509th Bomb Wing station at Roswell Army Air Field and Major Jesse Marcel, the intelligence officer for the 509th as unable to tell a weather balloon form a flying saucer.

Now at that time in our military history, the 509th Bomb Wing was the most elite bombing wing on the planet having been the unit that dropped both atomic bombs on Japan to end World War II. Those assigned to this unit was said to be the best of the best, but they were made to look like fools by their chain of command. No one has been able to explain why General Ramey took that position. Well, time has revealed more answers.

It was Colonel Blanchard who had authorized Lieutenant Walter Haut to issue the press release that the 509th had recovered the wreckage of a flying saucer. This was after reviewing the debris collected by Major Marcel. Both of these very experience officers were convinced that the debris were not part of any conventional flying object. Additionally, knowing how the chain of command works, Colonel Blanchard would not have given the green light to the press release without checking with the command level of the Eighth Air Force.

After the press release hit the wire services, someone in Washington realized that this was no small matter being discussed in the press and that they had better get involved. It should be remembered that under the terms of the memo referencing Operation Majestic 12, the President was the final authority in regard to flying saucers. However, here was a subordinate unit of the Eighth Air Force releasing a press release that the United State Army Air Corp had a flying saucer.

According to General Ramey's Chief of Staff, Colonel Jefferson Dubose, he received a telephone call from General Clements McMullen, then Deputy Commander of the Strategic Air Command ordering that the story about finding the crashed disc be immediately killed. He further ordered that the crash debris be sent to him in Washington D.C. and he would personally have the debris put on his personal plane and flown to Wright Field in Dayton, Ohio.

It was as a result of these orders that General Roger Ramey put on the dog and pony show for the press to make his subordinates look like idiots for not being able to tell a weather balloon from a flying saucer[81].

After some suitable urging from the military, the story about the crashed disc fell off the headlines and was forgotten until 1978 when Stanton T. Friedman met Jesse Marcel who was retired and living in Houma, Louisiana. Then the story came out once again, this time without any military filters being in place[82]. An interplanetary craft crashed in Roswell, New Mexico[83].

The military immediately put out the cover story that the wreckage recovered at Roswell was nothing but a crashed weather balloon. However, as history as shown, as a direct result of this so-called crashed weather balloon, the

---

[81] Ibid

[82] It is interesting to note that having embarrassed the service with the press release, the careers of Colonel Blanchard and Major Marcel, not to mention a mere second lieutenant by the name of Walter Haut should have been in the toilet, but all three were promoted with Colonel Blanchard eventually reaching the four-star level prior to his death at his desk at the Pentagon. Clearly it was more than a weather balloon that came into the custody of the 509th back in July of 1947.

[83] As we shall see later, there is evidence that the military may have shot the craft down.

Air Force has been forced put out four very extensive, very expensive denials consisting of thousands of pages of mostly irrelevant material. These very elaborate denials have been written by the military and sold to the public denying that it was a flying saucer. Mostly, they are exercises in misdirection written by people whose job it is to put an end to the speculation, the truth be damned.

However, circumstantial evidence, alone, supports the premise that it was something very unique that was discovered by Major Jesse Marcel in the desert in 1947. Perhaps, something so unique that it shook the government to its basis.

CHAPTER ELEVEN
OTHER SIGHTINGS

Between the end of World War I, and the beginning of World War II, there were a number of sightings of mystery aircraft. Our watchers were still with us, keeping an eye on what we were doing. However, such was the state of news reporting, it being prior to cable television that there was very little solid news about these events.

During this interval there were also a number of stories about crashed UFOs being found by a number of countries. Supposedly the Nazis found one or two and the Italians recovered another that was given to the Nazis for study. However, there were no major breakthroughs in regard to technology that were widely reported.

During the 1930s there were several reports of either downed craft or craft that for various reasons had simply landed and they were not confined to the United States.

<u>IOWA</u>

The October 28, 1973 edition of the Hawk Eye Newspaper of Mount Pleasant, Iowa included a very unusual submission by resident Clark Linch. Mr. Linch was 75 years old at the time, and a had a very unusual story to relate from his youth. According to Mr. Linch, the story took place in 1920.

According to Mr. Linch, this story took place about 10:30 in the morning on the 3rd day of June 1920. He had been out fishing when he had encountered what he believed was an extraterrestrial craft[84]. He said he was sitting quietly on the riverbank when this egg-shaped device landed about 15 feet from where he was fishing. He did not know what to

---

[84] When asked how he had remembered the event as well as the specific date, he replied that it happened on his birthday and he had gotten married in January of that year. Two hard to forget events.

INTERVENTION 141

do so he simply sat there watching the device. It made no hospital actions toward him and eventually it took off and vanished into the sky[85].

PAKISTAN

It was reported that in 1923, a UFO exploded over the tow of Quetta, Pakistan. Flaming debris rained down over the town and even destroyed a few buildings. The fire that consumed the crashed object burned for hours before leaving only melted slag and some thin wires to show for the incident[86].

AUSTRALIA

In 1930, a report came from Mandurah, West Australia. According to the story told by the farmer, a small humanoid showed up at his door asked for water. The farmer frightened by what he believed to be an alien shot the creature[87].

---

[85] Carlson, Gil, UFO Crashes, Retrievals and Government Coverups: An Encyclopedia of UFOs Crashes, Wicked Wolf Press.
[86] Ibid
[87] Ibid

CANADA

One of the most interesting came from the community of Nipawin in Saskatchewan, Canada. According to the three witnesses, during the Summer of 1933, there had been a number of stories circulating throughout the community that some homesteaders and at least one forest tower ranger had reported seeing some very strange lights in the sky[88]. Most of the locals believed that these stories were false, but three individuals, two men and a woman, drove out to the area where the lights and been seen in order to find out for themselves if the stories were true or not.

Arriving in the area, the saw a mysterious glow coming from a nearby area. When they approached the location, they discovered that the road was blocked by a very marshy area, so they got out of their vehicle and hiked toward the area where the glow seemed to be originating.

---

[88] Ufoevidence.org

Arriving, they discovered that the glowing lights were coming from a large oval shaped object sitting in a clearing in the middle of the marshland. In later discussions, they all agreed that it was a large craft, domed on the top and slightly rounded on the bottom.

The craft was sitting up on legs and there were about a dozen figures that could be seen entering and leaving the craft through a hatch that was reached by a ladder like stairway. The figures seemed to be in the process of working on or repairing their craft.

GERMANY

Over the years there have been many stories about the Nazis having recovered either one or even several UFOs from crash sites. Whether or not these stories are true, one story that generated a lot of interest originated in the Black Forest area of Germany.

According to this story, in 1936, in the Black Forest area of Germany a crashed UFO was discovered. According to writer, John Von Helsing, members of the Vril tried to back engineer the craft. The project, which had Nazi support, was called the Haunebu and allegedly led to the development of a German flying saucer[89].

POLAND

In the summer of 1938, a UFO crashed in the area near Jelenia Gora. According to several Soviet and Russian authors the wreckage that was recovered from the site by the Polish authorities was seized by the Germany military during the German invasion of Poland in 1939. It was reported that from this wreckage, Nazi scientists constructed the V-7, also called the disco plane[90].

So, based on the reporting, there is little doubt that there were still UFO visitations in the years between the two great wars, though perhaps not as many, or perhaps they were just not seen as often. Having confirmed this, we will

---

[89] Carlson, Gil, UFO Crashes, Retrievals and Government Coverups: An Encyclopedia of UFOs Crashes, Wicked Wolf Press.
[90] Ibid

now move forward to review some of the sightings that came from the years of World War II.

CHAPTER TWELVE
THE BATTLE OF LOS ANGELES

Evidence seems to indicate that UFO sightings increase in number during periods of war. This is especially true during the era called World War II as we shall see. Of course, the question becomes is there more activity as a result of earthly war or are there more sightings simply because more people are watching the heavens in case of enemy attack? That is a question that is impossible to answer, but at the same time, some of the sightings are simply out of this world, so to speak.

December 7, 1941 was rightfully considered a day of infamy when the Japanese launched a surprise attack against our fleet in Pearl Harbor, Hawaii. After the fact, there were numerous stories told of residents seeing lights in the hills where there were supposed to be no inhabitants. Of course, the immediate explanations were that these lights were Japanese spies. Where they Japanese, or were they something else?

BATTLE OF LOS ANGELES

As a result of the Japanese attack on Pearl Harbor, the west coast of the United States was living in fear of the Japanese invading the mainland. Certainly, as unprepared as the U.S Military was at this point in time it would have been possible. In fact, the Imperial Japanese Army did invade and hold one or more islands in the Aleutian chain which was part of Alaska for more than a year. Japanese submarines also raided and even fired upon various installations on the west coast. It was a time of great fear.

At the time of this air raid, that has become known as the Battle of Los Angeles, the American forces in the Pacific were in disarray trying to defend against an unbroken string of defeats. There was anxiety on the home front and even Congress, normally in possession of all of the answers, was uncertain of what to do next. In fact, on February 24, 1942, U.S. Naval Intelligence had issued a warning that a Japanese attack on Los Angeles could be expected within the next 10 hours[91]. There were also a lot of blinking lights and flares seen around some of the defense plans that ringed Los Angeles. Some of the older people remembered the rash of mystery aircraft that seemed to be attacking defense plants on the east coast both before and during World War I.

To make matters worse, at the same time that President Roosevelt was having one of his fireside chats on the radio, Japanese submarine I-17, commanded by Kozo Nishino[92], surfaced a few hundred yards off of the California coast less than ten miles down the coast from Santa Barbara

---

[91] Maloney, Mack, UFOs in Wartime: What They Didn't Want You To Know, Berkley Books, New York 2011.
[92] Joseph, Frank, Military Encounters with Extraterrestrials: The Real War of the Worlds, Bear and Company, Rochester, VT. And Toronto, Canada.

and fired approximately twenty-five 5.5 inch shells at the Ellwood Oil Fields, destroying a derrick, a pump house and doing other damage described as minor. The real damage by this attack was to public morale that a Japanese sub could actually shell the homeland[93] and escape unharmed. Though the I-17 cruised slowly up and down that section of the coast, not one single shot was fired at the Japanese Submarine[94] until it submerged and headed for Japan, the victor in this odd little engagement.

It was certainly interesting that the 4th Interceptor Command of the U.S. Army Air Corps sent no planes against the I-17 even though they were well aware of the submarine's activities and its location. The only action taken by anyone at the time was to order a blackout that extended from Ventura to Goleta. This complete lack of response by the military was an additional blow to civilian morale.

---

[93] Ibid
[94] Collins, Paul T., The Battle of Los Angeles, Fate 17, no 322, July 1987.

Then another Japanese Submarine, the I-25, commanded by Mejil Tagami, dodged a protective minefield by following a group of American fishing boats, near the mouth of the Columbia River in Oregon to surface some ten miles from Fort Stevens. This time the submarine fired a total of 17 shells at Battery Russell which was part of Fort Stevens. The primary casualty of the backstop at the fort's baseball diamond, though shell fragments did damage some power and telephone lines which were quickly repaired. Under orders not to give away their position, the Battery failed to return fire once again.

Three months later, the I-25 returned for another crack at causing major damage to the American Homeland. On September 9, 1942, the I-25 launched its seaplane off the Oregon coast with orders to drop two incendiary bombs in the heavily forested areas of beyond the coast. Luckily a forest ranger spotted the fire and its was quickly extinguished.

As if this was not bad enough, the already concerned citizens of Los Angeles were rudely awakened at 3:16 am on the morning of February 25, 1942, when the peace of the night was shattered by the shrill wail of air raid sirens and every artillery piece and anti-aircraft gun stationed in and around that city opened fire at much the same time. The thought in the mind of every civilian was that the Japanese were invading. Mass confusion was the order of the day.

Of course, over the years there have been a number of things written about what has come to be called the Battle of Los Angeles. Many people firmly believe it is a hoax, others believe that, if anything really happened, it was the Japanese. However, the evidence is rather clear, something did happen, but it was not the Japanese, by a long shot.

Almost before the shooting stopped, a total blackout was called form extending from Los Angeles to the Mexican Border and inland to the San Joaquin Valley[95]. It was a little

---

[95] Ibid

late, but it appeared to be better than nothing and did tend to sow that someone was at least in charge.

Though this was being viewed as an air raid, once gain the 4th Interceptor Command again sent up no planes. The protection of the entire Los Angeles was left in the hands of the anti-aircraft gunners. According to military records, by 4:14 am, the gunners fired over 1,500 rounds at the enemy planes. At 7:21 am, the all clear was sounded and the blackout was lifted.

A check of the area after dawn broke showed that a number of buildings and vehicles had been damaged by shell fragments and five persons were dead as a result of either heart failure or automobile accidents. According to the Glendale News Press, hundreds of civilians were scouring the vacant lots and streets in the area looking for souvenirs[96].

What was a surprise to many, however, was that in

---

[96] Harwood, Jeremy, Unexplained Mysteries of World War II, Firefly Books, Buffalo, New York, 2014.

this "air raid" no bombs had been dropped and none of the enemy planes were shot down by the sheer mass of anti-aircraft fire. At a press conference, Secretary of the Navy Frank Knox called the event a false alarm. With Pearl Harbor such a recent memory, he called the incident just the result of war nerves.

As a precursor of the Roswell incident, public affairs officers for the United States Army Coast Artillery Association added their two cents worth calling the situation an unfortunate response to a weather balloon that had been mistaken for a Japanese bomber. The U.S. Air Force Historical Research Agency later repeated this the cause of the war fears that resulted in the Battle of Los Angeles[97].

In response to these reports, Lieutenant General John L. DeWitt, commander of the Army's Western Defense Command, insisted that the blackout and the anti-aircraft fire had been caused by unidentified targets sighted over the

---

[97] Ibid

beach area. Pilots of the unusually inactive 14th Interceptor Command stated that they were ordered to man their planes and await order to take off that never came. This was caused, they claimed, by reports of unknown intruders that were reported to be flying over the coastline.

The incident was reviewed at the highest levels of government. After a thorough investigation General George C. Marshall, Chief of Staff, was said to have sent a memo to President Roosevelt that *"regarding the air rad over Los Angeles. . . This headquarters had come to the determination that the mystery airplanes are, in fact, not earthly, and, according to secret intelligence sources, they are in all probability of interplanetary origin[98]."*

While Secretary of the Navy, Frank Knox was attributing the entire matter to war nerves and mass hysteria, the U.S. Army Command in San Francisco issues a

---

[98] George C. Marshall, top-secret memo to the president, in UFO Quotes, MUFON Pennsylvania, West Virginia.

statement confirming (and later a second statement that reconfirmed) that there were, in fact, unidentified aircraft over southern California. Confirmation was also received from the 37th Coast Artillery Brigade that they had begun firing 50 caliber machine guns rounds and 12.8-pound anti-aircraft shells at what they confirmed was a solid target. The gunners also claimed that they hit this solid at least twice without any visible effect[99].

Further confirmation that there was at least one solid target over the city was forthcoming from the 65th Coast Artillery Regiment stationed in Inglewood and the 205th Artillery Regiment (Anti-aircraft), which was based in Santa Monica. Gunners from each of these units also claimed that they also saw a solid target and claimed to have hit the target.

Supporting the military were the local news outlets. Bill Henry of the *Los Angeles Times* reported that he saw a

---

[99] Vander Ploeg, Dirk, The Untold Story of the Battle of Los Angeles, UFO Digest.

glowing object moving slowly over the area as the anti-aircraft batteries fired at it. He said that he was far enough away to see the object without being able to identify it and he was adamant that the gunners scored direct hits on the target which seemed to not be affected.

Another reporter for the *Los Angeles Times*, Marvin Wiles, wrote an article entitled "Chilly Throng Watches Shells Burst in the Sky." He wrote that the object was moving slowly across the city, but it was caught in the circle of lights like a hub if a bicycle surrounded by gleaming spokes[100].

A *Los Angeles Herald Express* staffer wrote that he was sure that many of the shells had hit the target. He expressed amazement that the craft had not been shot down. He further reported that the object proceeded at a leisurely pace over the coastal cities between Santa Monica and Long

---

[100] Sword, Terrenz, The Battle of Los Angeles, 1942: The Mystery Air Raid (Seattle: Create-Space, 2010).

Beach, taking over thirty minutes to travel about twenty miles[101].

In addition to the military affirmations that there was at least one solid air craft over Los Angeles that night, there were also tens of thousands of civilians with binoculars also scanning the sky, that reported the craft.

There was also a coast artillery Colonel who spotted what he claimed to be twenty-five planes at twelve thousand feet over Los Angeles. Additionally, as soon as the blackout went into effect, the military information center was inundated with calls reporting enemy planes flying over the city. Later the Army issued a War Department report indicating that between one and five unidentified objects had flown over the city that night[102].

---

[101] Collins, Paul T., The Battle of Los Angeles, Fate 17, no 322, July 1987.
[102] Sword, Terrenz, "The Battle of Los Angeles, 1942: The Mystery Air Raid" (Seattle: Create-Space, 2010).

By dawn those senior government officials who were concerned about how things looked, became concerned that since the Army gunners had not been able to bring down this alleged slow-moving weather balloon in the hour they shot at it, such a public display of incompetence would further depress civilian morale. As a result, they issued a report that the defenders of Los Angeles had been decided by a meteorological phenomenon of some kind. In response, Secretary of War, Henry Stimson declared that approximately fifteen planes had doubtless violated southern California airspace.

It turned out that the military had built several highly classified radar installations in the southern California area and these classified facilities had tracked a number of unknown targets approaching at about twelve thousand feet over the sea, approximately 120 miles off the west coast at 2:15 am on February 25, 1942.

Further, within a few minutes after the alarm was sounded, ground observers were reporting an enormous, luminous object flying slowly over the city[103]. These observations were further confirmed by non-military witnesses, many using binoculars.

Peter Jenkins, editor of the *Los Angeles Herald Examiner* reported clearly seeing a V formation o about twenty-five, silvery planes flying overhead, moving slowly across the sky toward Long Beach[104]. J. H. McClelland, the police chief in Long Beach, watched what was described as the second wave of planes from the top of the seven story Long Beach City Hall[105].

An experienced Navy observer using very powerful field glasses reported he counted nine silver colored planes in the cone of the searchlight. (It should be noted here that

---

[103] Randle, Kevin D., The UFO Dossier: One Hundred Years of Government Secrets, Conspiracies, and Cover-ups (Canton, MI: Visible Ink, 2015)
[104] The Institute for the Study of Globalization and Covert Politics, "Battle of Los Angeles, Recent Testimony."
[105] Ibid

the Japanese did not use silver colored aircraft, but rather camouflage.)

Tracking the reports shows that these mystery aircraft went from one battery of searchlights to another, all the while under fire from antiaircraft batteries. They were tracked from the area of Redondo Beach and Inglewood to the landward side of Fort MacArthur, and in the direction of Santa Ana and Huntington Beach[106].

In the aftermath of this incident there was a lot of finger pointing, of course, but also lot of activity behinds the scenes. The top-secret memo written by General George C. Marshall referenced previously also went on to say that *"it was learned by Army G2 that Rear Admiral Walter Stratton[107] recovered an unidentified airplane off the coast of California . . .with no bearing on conventional explanation."*

---

[106] Joseph, Frank, Military Encounters with Extraterrestrials: The Real War of the Worlds, Bear and Company, Rochester, VT. And Toronto, Canada.
[107] 1881-1981

And finally, it was alleged by Dr. Michael Wolf, of MJ 12 fame in a conversation with Richard Boylan, Ph.D. that the first UFO came down in 1941 into the ocean west of San Diego and was retrieved by the Navy. He went on to say that the Navy has held a leadership position in UFO matters ever since[108]. So, it seems that by sometime in 1941, the Navy had the ability to recover UFOs so if one of the air craft, that was clearly flying over Los Angeles during the so-called Battle of Los Angeles, did sustain damage and crash into the ocean, the Navy would have been able to retrieve it.

However, to return to the air raid, the question becomes, what was it that was flying over Los Angeles on that night in February 1942? Witnesses reported aircraft, those who were nowhere near the site called it war nerves. Who was correct?

---

[108] Carlson, Gil, UFO Crashes, Retrievals and Government Coverups: An Encyclopedia of UFOs Crashes, Wicked Wolf Press.

CHAPTER THIRTEEN
INCIDENTS WITH FOO FIGHTERS

The Foo Fighter period seemed to begin in either March or June of 1942 depending on which stories are studied. If we look at the pilots of these mystery craft as big brother, so to speak, it is clear that they were watching what we were doing, especially during time of war. The question is why were they paying such close attention to our activities? The air raid over Los Angles was just the beginning of the activity that was reported during World War II.

The very first detailed report of a foo fighter was from Flight Lieutenant Roman Sabinski. He was a member of the 301st squadron of a Polish division attached to the

RAF. The incident happened either March 25, 1942 or June 25, 1942 as there is no written report to refer to. At the time of the sighting, Sabinski was flying a Wellington Bomber over the Zuiderzee off of the coast of Holland when he was told that a strange looking craft was rapidly gaining on them. Since they were returning from a bombing mission over Germany, the crew was certain it was a German air craft.

When the strange craft got to within 200 yards of Sabinski's bomber, his tail gunner open fired on the stranger, but though he could tell that his rounds hit the circular craft, they were having no noticeable effect. The mysterious craft seemed to be content to simply fly alongside of Sabinski's plane. In spite of numerous attempts by the gunners to shoot the disk down, none of their rounds had any effect on the stranger. Eventually, it flew off, showing much greater speed than the Wellington[109].

---

[109] Maloney, Mack, UFOs in Wartime: What They Didn't Want You to Know, Berkley Books, New York, 2011.

In the early hour of June 6, 1944, also known as D-Day, the U.S. Eighth Air Force launched approximately 13,000 war planes against the German Forces occupying defensive emplacements in France. A report from a veteran who wished to remain anonymous, who served aboard a B-17 heavy bomber, discussed an encounter with one of the mysterious foo fighters[110]. According to his statement as the B-17 approached its target, some ten minutes after they crossed the coast, one of the fighter escorts radioed that there were bandits at 6 o'clock high. This veteran was a waist-gunner on the right side of the plane. He went to cock his weapon and it jammed. The weapon looked perfectly normal, but it simply refused to function[111].

At about that same time, the veteran saw the bandits approaching and he said that they were like no fighter planes

---

[110] Joseph, Frank, Military Encounters with Extraterrestrials: The Real War of the Worlds, Bear and Company, Rochester, VT. And Toronto, Canada.
[111] Anonymous, "France, Tuesday, June 6, 1944," UFO Hunters, October 30, 2009.

he had ever seen. They were luminous spheres that bore no insignia. He also noticed that at about the same time his gun jammed, the electrical systems on board the B-17 ceased to function. The radio went out and the number 4 engine stalled and ceased to function as well.

With one engine not functioning the B-17 could not keep up with the formation and had to drop out of place which made it a perfect target for German interceptors. As the B-17 slowed down, the luminous foo fighter[112] sped up and took off at what was described as an exceptionally high speed. Approximately fifteen minutes later, the waist-gunner's .50 caliber unjammed itself[113], the radio began to function once again and the inoperative engine number 4 began to run smoothly once more. This particular B-17 lived

---

[112] The name foo fighter was a pun on the French word feu, which meant fire and came from the popular comic of the time, Smokey Stover.
[113] Frankly, an impossible occurrence as anyone who has worked with the .50 caliber can tell you. When it is jammed, it has to be taken apart to unjam.

to fly another day but all allied craft targeted by the mysterious foo fighters were not so lucky.

On September 6, 1943, during a raid on Stuttgart, the 384th Group found itself proceeding between 2,000 and 3,000 feet beneath and behind five Luftwaffe aircraft[114]. Before either side could take any aggressive movements against the other, a cluster of small, round silvery objects fell from the sky above the Bombers of the 384th. The American pilots were adamant that these mysterious spheres did not come from the German planes.

These objects fell onto the wing of a B-17 heavy bomber in the group and it immediately began to burn. Pilots reported that this particular B-17 fell to earth like a comet and apparently crashed. If this was intentional hostile action by these mysterious watchers, then the ten-man crew on this

---

[114] Joseph, Frank, Military Encounters with Extraterrestrials: The Real War of the Worlds, Bear and Company, Rochester, VT. And Toronto, Canada.

particular B-17 were the first reported casualties in what might be termed a war of the worlds[115].

There may well have been more or even earlier hostile actions against allied aircraft but, if so, these were never reported. As became the norm, senior Army Air Corps Commanders forbid discussions about such encounters. Now some of them may have truly thought that such reports were the result of battle fatigue, fear, altitude sickness, weather conditions or even enemy secret weapons. However, there were so many such reports that it became clear that there was something weird taking place in the skies over the battlefield.

During the last two years of the war, there were hundreds of such reports coming from all combat theaters. Naturally, there were probably hundreds of other reports

---

[115] Randle, Kevin D., The UFO Dossier: One Hundred Years of Government Secrets, Conspiracies, and Cover-ups (Canton, MI: Visible Ink, 2015)

never made due to the fear of pilots that they would be punished for reporting what they saw.

THE EASTERN FRONT

Reports of these mysterious air craft were not just limited to the Western European Theater of operations, there were numerous reports filtering out of what was called the Eastern Front as well. While the luminous Foo Fighter was common, there were many other types of mystery aircraft overflying the battlefields of the world. A prime example came from the Battle of Kursk.

On July 4, 1943, just as the pivotal Battle of Kursk began, a huge silvery disk was seen hovering over the opposing forces, though it did not take a direct part in the battle. After a short period of time, the massive disk just vanished. Naturally, the Soviet High Command was terrified that this disk was one of Hitler's secret weapons.

Russian born writer and researcher, Paul Stonehill collected what information was available about this sighting.

There were, unfortunately, no photographs taken of this hovering disk, but a detailed drawing of it was made and signed by several Soviet colonels who later took part in the Battle of Kursk[116].

On August 26, 1943, three days after the conclusion of the Battle of Kursk, Senior Lieutenant Gennady Zhelaginova of the Red Army reported seeing a sickle shaped craft fly over the battlefield at tremendous speed. He said that the craft came in low over an area of the battlefield that hi artillery had targeted. He also noted that the craft was dark blue overall but with a bright orange center section[117].

It was also interesting to note that the Soviet Air Defense units fired on this mystery craft with everything they could bring to bear, but nothing seemed to have any effect on the strange aerial object. This incident was also reported by Soviet Colonel Gherman Kolchin in the 2000

---

[116] Stonehill, Paul, The Soviet UFO Files, Bramley Books, UK, 1998.
[117] Ibid

issue of New Literary Observer, the oldest Russian independent magazine specializing in philology, cultural history and historical anthropology[118].

It should also be kept in mind that the Russians, like their western comrades initially thought that these strange flying objects were some new type of German secret weapon. No one, at the time, considered that they could be extraterrestrial in nature.

Pilots in the American, British and the Russian air forces were warned the keep quiet about that they saw in the air. The official view was to stop any type of investigation and to stop it cold. Officially, nothing but military planes were in the air and if it meant ruining a few careers to stop any discussions about these disks, then so be it[119].

---

[118] Ibid
[119] Crowe, Harre, "Project 1944, UFO Reports 1944,"

THE GERMAN VIEW

While most of the allied pilots believed that these strange craft soaring over the battlefield were German secret weapons, the pilots of the Luftwaffe thought that the lights might be an allied secret weapon. Clearly, the German air force had no better idea than did the allies what these UFOs represented,

There was no question that the Germans were ahead of the allies in regard to research on advanced aircraft, certainly their best efforts were no match for the mystery aircraft. On February 3, 1942, Germany's premier test pilot Hanna Reitsch took off in the world's first operational rocket powered fighter plane. According to what Hanna Reitsch wrote in her biography she was putting the still experimental Messerschmitt 163A *Komet* through its paces, climbing at 525 feet per second and had reached seven and a half miles almost straight up into the sky when a silvery disk shot past her as if she was standing still. The mystery air craft reached

60,000 feet, above the maximum ceiling of the Komet and hovered before vanishing in the sky almost instantly[120].

Though the allies had come into contact with the Foo Fighters in 1942, apparently, they had not become a major issue with German pilots until the summer of 1944[121].

THE PACIFIC THEATER

These unusual air craft were not only being seen I the European and Russian Theaters, but in the Pacific Theater as well. The pilot of a B-29 Superfortress on its return flight from a bombing raid on the Pladjoe oil refinery at Palembang, Sumatra stated that not only his, but several other bomber crews, saw what they believed to be a new type of weapon and then went on to describe a foo fighter. One of the B-29s was under attack by a foo fighter for over an hour and ten minutes.

---

[120] Reitsch, Hanna, Flying is My Life, G. P. Putnam, New York, 1954
[121] Stevens, Henry, Hitler's Flying Saucers, Adventures Unlimited, Kempton, IL, 2015.

He also went on to state that at one point during the flight, the course was altered in order to allow the tail gunners to fire in the direction of these mysterious luminous craft, but the fire had no visible effect on the mysterious air craft[122].

On November 3, 1944, nine Mitchell B-25 Medium bombers assigned to the 10th Air Force in Burma conducted a raid on target in Japanese held China. While attacking the bridge approached at Hsenwi, Namhkai and Kawnghka, all nine of the B-29s were surrounded by an undetermined number of glittering objects. The bombers all experienced complete instrument failure and loss of power to their engines. The bombers tried to fight back, but the foo fighters were moving so quickly and erratically that no one could track them much less take a shot at them. Only after the

---

[122] Joseph, Frank, Military Encounters with Extraterrestrials: The Real War of the Worlds, Bear and Company, Rochester, VT. And Toronto, Canada.

objects broke off their attack did the electrical systems and the engines return to normal[123].

As strange as the encounters were between allied air craft and these mystery craft, it was not just the air crews that had strange experiences to talk about. So to, did the men of the Navy.

---

[123] "The Foo Fighters of World War II," www.saturdaynightuforia.

CHAPTER FOURTEEN
NAVAL ENCOUNTERS

It has not been just aerial encounters that has shown that there are others besides the human race occupying this planet. There have been numerous encounters between UFOs and Naval aviators and ships, especially during wartime. We will look at a few of the oddest that were reported.

HAWAII

According to Japanese records, their airmen had been photographing UFOs for almost five years before allied pilots in the European theatre of operations encountered what they called foo fighters. There is also a report that after the bombing of Pearl Harbor on December 7, 1941, the

Japanese carrier based B5N torpedo bombers that had led the attack on the Pacific fleet were given a UFO escort on their return flight to their carrier bases.

In fact, most of the Japanese contacts with what we might call foo fighters were very non-violent until April 24, 1946 at the Genzan Air Group Base in Wonsan, Korea. One afternoon, ground observers saw an unidentifiable aircraft approaching the base. These unidentifiable aircraft were later identified as two silver disks, each said to be approximately 100 feet in diameter.

A trio of A6M2b Zeros were scrambled and closed with the incoming strangers. The Japanese pilots immediately began to fire their twin 20-millimeter canons at the saucer shaped craft. One of the UFO appeared damaged, but it remained aloft. The other UFO shone a bright beam of light at the closest Zero which immediately pun out of control and crashed into the sea. Both UFOs immediately accelerated and rapidly outran the Zeros[124].

RNN TROMP

In February 1942 the Dutch cruiser RNN *Tromp* was patrolling in the Timor Sea, close to New Guinea. A lookout saw a huge saucer shaped object that he estimated to be a mile high approaching the ship at a tremendous speed[125]. As the lookout watched, the saucer shaped craft slowed its speed and began to circle the cruiser. In fact, it circled the cruiser for over four hours, maintaining the same altitude and speed the entire time. Finally, it left at a speed estimated to be approximately Mach 5.

TASMANIA

During the Summer of 1942, a Royal Australian Air Force pilot had a bit of a shock. He was flying over Tasmania when he encountered a mysterious aircraft he said was

---

[124] 1945: January UFO ad Alien Sightings. Thinkaboutitdocs.com
[125] Maloney, Mack, UFOs in Wartime: What They Didn't Want You To Know, Berkley Books, New York, 2011.

shaped like an airfoil. It was 150 log and approximately 50 feet wide. The object was bronze in color and had a dome on to. It was the pilot's impression that there was a helmeted figure sitting in the dome watching his plane.

The mystery aircraft kept pace with the Australian plane for a few minutes before turning away and accelerating at tremendous speed leaving a very baffled pilot behind.

SOLOMON ISLAND INVASION FORCE[126]

As the invasion fleet was constituted for the first major allied naval offensive in the Pacific, notice was served by the UFOs that they were a presence to be considered in regard to naval operations. On August 5, 1942, the men aboard the USS *Helm* went on alert as a result of a sighting of an unidentified air craft heading for their ship. A lookout using a 750-power set of binoculars identified the craft as a ninety-foot-wide craft, that was a silvery cigar shaped air craft topped by a round dome.

---

[126] Operation Watchtower, invasion of the Solomon Islands.

As the mystery air craft came into range, the anti-aircraft weapons of the USS Helm began to fire. Shortly these guns were joined by those of three nearby cruisers and seven destroyers that were also part of the invasion fleet. In spite of the veritable hail of anti-aircraft rounds, the mystery aircraft showed no visible damage[127].

Prior to leaving, the mystery aircraft made a complete circle around the invasion fleet at which time every ship began to fire it arsenal of weapons at the stranger. However, once again, there was no visible damage inflicted.

TULAGI

This is more evidence that active combat was something that these mysterious watchers had a great deal of interest in observing. Though it was the first offensive operation by the United States Navy against the Japanese, the invasion of the Solomon Islands was not a major focus

---

[127] Chester, Keith, Strange Company: Military Encounters With UFOs in World War II, Anomalist Books, 2010.

of World War II by any stretch of the imagination, but it had been the scene of heavy fighting.

On August 12, 1942, a Marine Sergeant was sitting in a foxhole on the island of Tulagi[128], one of the chain of islands in the Solomon Islands. The invasion of Tulagi had begun just a few days before on August 7, in an attempt to take the island away from a heavily dug in force of Japanese.

On this particular day, the final decision regarding whether the Marines or the Japanese would have final control of the island was still up for grabs. Combat had been hot and heavy, but on this morning, there was a modicum of calm. The Marines were sitting in their foxholes, resting and reading their equipment for a new round of combat. However, mid-morning, the air raid sirens began to wail.

Expecting another wave of Japanese planes to bomb their positions the Marines hunkered down deeply into their

---

[128] Tulagi was very close to Guadalcanal which had also been the scene of heavy fighting.

foxholes. However, instead of the sound of the Japanese planes that they had become accustomed to hearing, they heard a mighty roar that seemed to encompass the area.

Then, instead of the V shaped formations of Japanese planes, they saw wave after wave of bright silvery objects flying high overhead. It was later estimated that there were at least one hundred and fifty of these silvery craft. The Marines later agreed that the sight was simply awe inspiring[129].

There is every possibility that this was the UFO equivalent of a showing the flag mission. That is, showing the other side such undefeatable might that there is not even a battle. Of course, doing such a thing at a remote location such as Tulagi raises other questions. However, there is no doubt that the technology of these mysterious air craft was so advanced that in a pitched battle, the allied forces would

---

[129] Chester, Keith, Strange Company: Military Encounters With UFOs in World War II, Anomalist Books, 2010.

not have stood a chance. Perhaps this was the intent of the pilots of the UFOs, however, there was no confrontation, at least not one that received wide spread notice.

Another factor to consider was that there were numerous crashes at sea during World War II and of course, Naval units were vectored to the last reported locations of these air craft only to find nothing. However, it is interesting to note that though the crashed planes were, many times, not found, unexplained radar sightings were often seen in the area of the purported crash. Many senior military commanders thought that there might be a connection between the missing planes and he unexplained radar contacts.

Though there were a tremendous number of sightings during the war, as we shall see, the end of the war did not bring an end to the sightings.

CHAPTER FIFTEEN
THE GHOST ROCKETS

With the end of World War II, the population of the world expected to have peace for at least a few years. However, this was not to be, as there was immediately a new threat – the Ghost Rockets.

This new possible threat to the world made its appearance in the northern reaches of Scandinavia. For the most part, the mysterious foo fighters vanished with the end of the war, but now these new mysterious craft were being seen throughout the Scandinavian arctic. However, this time these intruders were not mystery airplanes but rather rockets that were seen streaking across the frigid skies of Sweden, Norway and Finland. Unlike the so-called ghost flyers of 1934, these rockets were seen by many people to include military pilots. These mystery rockets were seen during daylight hours and o some days there were literally hundreds of reports[130].

With the advances in news reporting achieved during World War II, unlike the skimpy reporting of the Ghost Flyers in 1934, the news coverage of the Ghost Rockets was splashed across the newspapers of the world.

The first sightings of the Ghost Rockets took place in 1946. Beginning with just a few reports of these mysterious aircraft, soon there were literally hundreds of reports from all over the country. Initially, the descriptions consisted of balls of light similar to the foo fighters of World War II, but soon most descriptions fell into two categories, a fast-moving rocket about 12-15 feet long with wings and a similar rocket without wings.

Naturally, the "experts" claimed that these lights in the sky were just meteors, and perhaps some were, but this

---

[130] Maloney, Mack, UFOs in Wartime: What They Didn't Want You To Know, Berkley Books, New York, 2011.

explanation was laughable when some of these lights were seen to fly horizontal, do 180 degree turns and on occasion fly in formation with other lights in the sky.

The Swedish government became so concerned about these Ghost Rockets that they asked the British to send them some of the latest radar equipment. Once installed and operational, the Swedes discovered that they were able to track over 200 of these mystery rockets.

Once again, Sweden reached out for help, this time to the United States. In answer to this plea for help, on August 20, 1946, General David Sarnoff[131] and Jimmy Doolittle, the leader of the first bombing attack on the homeland of Japan[132].

No government wanted to give the mysterious happenings any further publicity, so Sarnoff was supposedly in Sweden to study the market for broadcast equipment and

---

[131] David Sarnoff was a member of Dwight D. Eisenhower's wartime staff and went on to found RCA and NBC.
[132] This raid was known as the 30 Seconds Over Tokyo Raid. He was also a vice president of Shell Oil Company.

Doolittle was supposedly on an inspection tour of Shell facilities in the country[133].

After their inspection, the two returned to the United States where they reported their findings to the Central Intelligence Group (CIG) which later became the Central Intelligence Agency. Based on their information, the CIG prepared a report for President Truman wherein they identified the launching site for the mystery rockets – Peenemunde.

Of course, Peenemunde meant the Soviets as they had captured what had been the first rocket base on the planet. However, both Allied bombing and the Germans themselves had reduced the base to a burned-out ruin. Shortly after this, the ghost rockets simply vanished.

---

[133] Maloney, Mack, UFOs in Wartime: What They Didn't Want You To Know, Berkley Books, New York, 2011.

CHAPTER SIXTEEN
OPERATION HIGH JUMP

General Douglas MacArthur accepted the surrender of Imperial Japan on board the Battleship Missouri, September 2, 1945, officially ending World Wat II. However, it the world was officially at peace, then why was it that on August 26, 1946, a massive military armada departed the United States for the Antarctic.? By no stretch of the imagination could this be called a research expedition as it had some serious military firepower and a large complement of experienced personnel.

Though claimed to be a scientific expedition, Operation Highjump was carried out by thirteen warships supported by a flotilla of supply vessels, 112 aircraft and 4,700 servicemen. The flagship was the USS Philippine Sea one of the largest aircraft carrier ever built. Her air wing consisted of one hundred fighters, dive-bombers and torpedo bombers. She also carried 5-inch artillery and 40-millimeter Bofor anti-aircraft guns.

The screen for this might war machine were the destroyers USS Brownson and the USS Henderson as well as the USS Sennet, a very deadly submarine. Supporting these warships were the tankers USS Canisteo and USS Cacapon, plus the supply ships USS Merrick and the USS Yancey. Then there was the USS Mount Olympus, an amphibious force command ship with advanced communications equipment and extensive combat information spaces for large scale landing operations.

Leading the fleet through the icy waters were the icebreakers USS Burton Island and the USCGC Northwind. There were two seaplane tenders, the USS Pine Island and the USS Currituck. Also added to this might fleet was a Martin PBM Mariner and six Sikorsky H-5 Helicopters.

INTERVENTION

There were so many ships and aircraft that the fleet had to be divided into two segments, an eastern group and a western group. In overall command of what was called Task Force 68 was Admiral Richard E. Byrd, Jr.

The alleged purpose of Task Force 68 was the establishment of Little America IV, a research and training base in the Antarctic[134]. Even though Task Force 68 was a massive operation more aimed at an invasion than a peaceful research endeavor, the Government continually denied that there was any aggressive intent on the part of the expedition[135]. Of course, the mere fact that there were few research scientists and very little scientific equipment present was not commented on by the military. This was a primarily military operation.

---

[134] The initial report was entitled The United States Navy Antarctic Developments Program. The contents were rather vague in what the actual purpose of all of these preparations where actually for, but at one point it was mentioned that expedition was aimed at consolidating and extending United States sovereignty over the largest practicable area of the Antarctic continent. Later, this was denied by military authorities.
[135] Kearns, David A., Operation Highjump: Task Force 68: Where Hell Freezes Over; A Story of Amazing Bravery and Survival, Thomas Dunne, New York, 2005.

On January 15, 1947, the armada landed personnel at the Bay of Whales. Work was started at once on building a headquarters, called Little America IV. Frankly, this was the only one of the announced expedition goals accomplished. Though this expedition was originally scheduled to last between six and eight months, just forty days later, Task Force 68 began withdrawing toward South America for what was announced as necessary repairs. Their destination was Chile.

Even though they were on the Antarctic continent for some forty days, the aircraft of Task Force 68 logged 220 hours of flight time and covered 22,700 miles, an area half the size of the United States. Over 70,000 reconnaissance photos were taken ore of which are still classified to this day.

Even the repairs needed by the various ships in the armada were considered very strange and they were quite extensive, appearing more like damage that would have come from combat operations and not a scientific expedition.

The mainstream press in Chile immediately picked upon the fact that something very odd had happened to the armada while in Antarctica. Adding to the confusion was an interview that Admiral Byrd himself had given to reporter Van Atta of the El Mercurio, Chile's largest newspaper on March 5, 1947.

According to Van Atta's story, Admiral Byrd warned that it was imperative that the United States initiate immediate defense measures against hostile forces threatening form the Arctic or the Antarctic. He said he was not trying to unduly alarm anyone, but the cruel reality was that in case of a new war, the United States could be attacked by flying objects which could move from pole to pole at incredible speed.

On his return to Washington, Admiral Byrd was interviewed by Security Service officials after which he never uttered another word about Operation Highjump. At the same time the entire operation was classified, thereby legally preventing its veterans from ever discussing what had happened.

In the reports subsequently issued and though it was glossed over, it was clear the Admiral Byrd's fleet had lost half of its seaplane and helicopter force. Admiral Byrd's plane had vanished for over three hours, but when he finally returned, it had not run out of fuel, though it should have done so. The reports admitted that there had been a number of casualties, but it was claimed that they were all due to accidents.

Clearly, the American public was not given the truth about what took place during operation Highjump. There were many stories that have circulated over the years that Admiral Byrd's forces met a force that, in spite of his invasion level fleet, handed him several defeats before he pulled his forces out after only 40 days.

SOVIET KNOWLEDGE OF TASK FORCE 68

At this late date it should certainly be no surprise that a number of Democratic Congressmen during World War II were actually Soviet agents. One was Samuel Dickstein of New York who was a close friend of President Roosevelt. He and others of his political persuasion funneled classified information to the Soviets, so they had more information about what happened than did the American people.

According to the records in the possession of the Soviets, two days after making land fall at the Bay of whales, the Americans saw lights on the horizon. Nearly three hours later, the lights reappeared in the same area and began to rapidly close on the USS Brownson. As they approached the commander of the Brownson gave the order to fire every air defense weapon on board began to fire at the intruders without achieving any hits. This encounter was alleged to have begun a series of brief but fierce skirmishes that lasted over the next several weeks between the ships of Task Force

68 and the lights which resulted in dozens of officers and men killed or wounded[136].

It is sad that the American public has to learn the truth about Operation Highjump from the Soviets, but it would seem that the military did not want anyone to know that the most powerful country in the world got its collective ass kicked by an unknown force with technology far beyond that available to the American military. Such a sad commentary. The only bright spot, if you will, was that the USS Sennet managed to get off a lucky shot and down one of the UFOs using its deck gun[137].

These stories do go hand in hand with the many stories of the secret German Base 100 that the German Navy supposedly built for Hitler in the closing days of World War II. Germans or aliens, who controls the Antarctic?

---

[136] Joseph, Frank, Military Encounters with Extraterrestrials: The Real War of the Worlds, Bear and Company, Rochester, VT. And Toronto, Canada.
[137] Ibid

CHAPTER SEVENTEEN
THE COLD WAR YEARS

In the aftermath of World War II, the United States and its wartime ally the Soviet Union became deadly enemies. At the same time, the military continued to assure the American people that UFOs did not exist. After all, if you couldn't believe your own government, then who could you believe?

Of course, there were signs that we were being lied to. An article in the Los Angeles Times by reporter Darrell Garwood read "*Jets Told to Shoot Down Flying Discs. Air Force Puzzled but No Longer Skeptical.*" The crux of the story told by this Washington DC reporter was that he had interviewed a United States Air Force Major who had confirmed that his orders to fire on UFOs were not rumors.

All jet pilots had been told to approach and fire on any of the UFOs they might encounter[138].

In spite of everything however, Americans have slept secure in the knowledge that we have an arsenal of missiles to protect us against a Soviet attack. However, what would have happened to this feeling of security if it became known that at any given time, some of our missiles may have been useless?

During what might be referred to as the Cold War, the most powerful segment of the military was naturally the USAF Strategic Air Command (SAC). These were the men and planes that would head out to destroy the enemy if the United States was attacked and it also controlled all of the ICBM missiles in the military arsenal. Offutt Field, the headquarters of SAC is, naturally one of the most secure

---

[138] Ibid

spots on the planet. That is why what happened on September 8, 1958 was considered so bizarre[139].

According to the reports, what at first appeared to be a jet contrail morphed until it was a visible cigar shaped object hovering above the field. Then it released hundreds of small black flecks that flew in every direction. Shortly thereafter, the cigar shaped object faded from view.

The missiles in America's nuclear arsenal were known as Minutemen and they were spread among a number of missile silos in Missouri, Montana, North Dakota, South Dakota and Wyoming. Each missile silo was connected to a missile control room that was staffed 24 hours a day. There were also a cadre of external guards. Each silo was situated many miles from the next closest silo. Their very location was a closely guarded secret.

---

[139] Maloney, Mack, UFOs in Wartime: What They Didn't Want You To Know, Berkley Books, New York, 2011.

At the height of their expansion there were dozen major ICBM bases in all and to the surprise of everyone, each of these bases had received visits from UFOs[140].

At least four times, UFOs were reported hovering over the Hanford Engineering Works in Hanford, Washington, the location of America's first nuclear reactor. There have been reports of UFOs hovering over Oak Ridge, Tennessee, and Los Alamos, New Mexico as well as other nuclear facilities.

THE FIRST INCIDENT

The very first incident that gave rise to a lot of concern took place at a nuclear silo under construction near Oracle, Arizona not too far from Davis-Monthan Air Force Base. According to the story, a workman saw a bright light hovering over a not yet completed silo and notified the base. Two interceptors were scrambled and sent to the scene, but

---

[140] Ibid

the light vanished as they approached only to reappear as if from nowhere when they left.

MORE SIGHTINGS

In 1962, Walker Air Force Base in New Mexico received its first ICBM. Within a year, reports were coming out of the base about UFOs either hovering or overflying the base. Though these reports were sent to higher headquarters numerous times, no action was taken, as if higher headquarters simply did not care or were ordered not to investigate[141]. In fact, there have been so many strange things seen by security personnel and odd happenings at Walker Air Force Base that some guards expressed that they were afraid to patrol around the silos at night[142].

Then there is Warren Air Force Base located just outside Cheyenne, Wyoming. Warren is one of the oldest military installations in the country having begun as a

---

[141] Ibid
[142] Walker Air Force Base was originally known as Roswell Army Airfield.

cavalry fort in 1867. It is also one of the largest nuclear missile bases in the world.

On August 1, 1965, there were eleven confirmed UFO sightings on or over Warren Air force Base. On another occasion, base security personnel saw 8 lights hovering over another silo. That same night NORAD admitted to tracking those same eight lights, though later the base commander denied everything.

Then there were the very strange happenings at Whitman Air Force Base located just outside of Kansas City, Missouri. During the 196-s, there was huge ICBM complex at Whitman that contained approximately 150 missiles, about ten percent of our ready reaction force. According to a report given to NUFORC beginning at about 9:00 PM on the night of June 16, 1966, a saucer shaped craft over flew the base.

As this mysterious craft flew over a missile silo, all electricity to that particular silo stopped, making it impossible to launch the missile contained in that silo. Electricity returned when the UFO left the immediate area of the effected silo.

What was so strange was that this saucer shaped craft spent the next two hours flying over each silo in turn until it had killed the power in all 150 silos. Finally, it flew off and electricity returned to all of the effected silos.

There is a laundry list of similar situations where UFOs were able to deactivate nuclear missiles. Frankly such an ability makes this a real danger to the country, whether the enemy is the Soviet Union or the UFOs themselves. Evidence has made it very clear that they have a major interest in our nuclear testing, even flying on the edge of test explosions at various test sites around the world. So, the question becomes why are they involving themselves in something that is clearly none of their business?

It also coincides with the warnings that UFO contactees were receiving that earth should stop its nuclear testing.

<u>THIS IS NOT A TEST</u>

Probably the most concerning occurrence took place at Minot Air Force Base in North Dakota. In the 1960s this base was the home to not only a large contingent of ICBM missiles but also a wing of B-52 bombers.

In July of 1967, base security spotted a large bright object flying over the Minot missile range. Other reports indicated that this object was flying from silo to silo. Within an hour all of the Minot's launch facilities. Then as the UFO was passing over one of the silos, warning indicators showed that a launch was in progress. The passage of this UFO over one of the silos had activated the launch sequence.

Luckily the control room personnel were able to stop the launch sequence, but what if they had not? It was readily apparent that the UFO had probed the missiles controls and activated it. When reported to the base commander, the response was surprising. Officially, nothing had happened[143].

---

[143] Ibid

CHAPTER EIGHTEEN
THE SECRECY

It is understandable that the military does not want any discussion about losing control of nuclear missiles, but to punish members of the military for reporting these odd occurrences is idiocy itself. There is also the question of just how far senior members of our government will go in the efforts to continue this cover-up.

An example of just how fanatical some official became about the secrecy that was put into place regarding UFOs can be seen in regard to the Forrestal Affair[144]. James Vincent Forrestal was the Secretary of the Navy in the later part of World War II and was later promoted to the Secretary

---

[144] It was allegedly Forrestal's plan that brought down the UFO at Roswell.

of Defense. He was a strong believer that the American people should be made aware of the danger the country faced because of the UFOs.

On September 23, 1947, Forrestal arrived at his new job at the Pentagon. He also received a newly completed report entitled *"Air Material Command Opinion Concerning Flying Discs."* According to author Tony Brunt, this document was prepared by a panel of sixteen military and civilian appointees in the wake of the Roswell crash. The report ended by recommending that an Operation called Majestic 12 was to be undertaken as a fully funded and operational Top-Secret Research and Development intelligence gathering agency to deal with the UFO issues.

This recommendation was approved by Truman and Forrestal was instructed to begin funding and organizing the MJ 12 program. He followed his orders but from the very beginning of Majestic 1s, Secretary Forrestal opposed the continued secrecy and suppression of information regarding an extraterrestrial presence on this planet. He was strongly opposed by the other members of MJ 12 who argued that the knowledge would completely unhinge society. As a result of his strong opposition to what was taking place, he resigned not only from MJ 12 but also as Secretary of Defense on March 28, 1949[145].

According to rumor, he joined forces with his friend Admiral Richard E. Byrd to determine a way to make the public aware of the danger represented by UFOs. However, his initial efforts to contact people who could help him, resulted in agents of President Truman finding out what he planned.

Whether with Truman's knowledge, or without it, Forrestal was taken into custody and confined to Bethesda Naval Hospital allegedly suffering from severe depression. On May 22, 1949, Forrestal allegedly fell to his death form

---

[145] Joseph, Frank, Military Encounters with Extraterrestrials: The Real War of the Worlds, Bear and Company, Rochester, VT. And Toronto, Canada.

the 16th floor of the National Naval Medical Center in Bethesda, Maryland. According to some reports, he had tied a sheet around his neck and attached it to the bed frame before jumping out the window. An official Navy Review Board called his death a suicide.

This decision stood until the late 1980s when photocopies of original U.S. government documents surfaced describing Operation Majestic 12. In related copies that appeared in later years, paragraph 11 stated that the untimely death of Secretary Forrestal was deemed necessary and regrettable[146].

So, this is the story. These mysterious craft have intervened in the development of the human race since time began. According to the Sumerian tablets translated by Zecharia Sitchin in the series the Earth Chronicles, they may have even had a hand in the development of the human race. Whatever may be the truth of this issue, one thing is clear,

---

[146] Wood, Robert M., Validating the New Majestic Documents.

they are watching over with a demonstrated technological level that far surpasses anything we have been able to develop. However, one thing is not clear, why are they going to such efforts to keep an eye on our development? What do they have to gain by doing so? Are they our saviors or our destroyers? Only time will tell.

INDEX

2

205th Artillery Regiment (Anti-aircraft), 156

3

37th Coast Artillery Brigade, 156

4

4th Interceptor Command, 150, 153

5

509th Bomb Wing, 134

6

65th Coast Artillery Regiment, 156
6th Massachusetts National Guard, 112

A

Abednego, 47
Abraham, Larry, 66
Adam, 30
Advanced Australopithecus, 15, 21
Akhenaten, 72, 91
Akkad, 42, 43
Aleutian chain, 148
Alexander the Great, 61
Allen, Gary, 66
Amon, 80
Angel of the Lord, 47
Angel Raphael, 87
Annunaki, 67, 88
Asmodeus, 87
Assyria, 81
Aten, 72
Attila the Hun, 49, 50

B

Babylon, 81
Battery Russell, 151
Battle of Kursk, 169, 170
Battle of Los Angeles, 4, 128, 130, 148, 150, 152, 154, 156, 157, 158, 160, 162
Battle of Milvian Bridge, 46
Battle of Mons, 85
Bay of Whales, 192
Berger, Joe, 112
Black Hand, 83
Book of Genesis, 30
Braidwood, Robert John, 29
Busby, Michael, 103
Byrd, Admiral Richard E., 191

C

Canaan, 35

Carlson, Gil, 141, 144, 162
Carneys Point, New Jersey, 116
Chester, Keith, 181, 183
Christianity, 45, 46, 50
Clark, Jerome, 94
Collins, Paul T., 150, 158
Constantine I, 45
Coslow, Richard, 57
Crenshaw, Dennis G., 106
Cro-Magnon, 21, 22, 25, 27, 41
Crowe, Harre, 171

D

Daily Mail, 99
Darwin, Charles, 13
Dash, Mike, 97
Dellschau, Charles A.A, 106
Dewey, John, 122
DeWitt, Lieutenant General John L., 154
Dickstein, Samuel, 195
Dobzhansky, Theodosius, 23
Doolittle, Jimmy, 187
Dorians, 35, 36, 37, 38, 39, 40, 41
Dubose, Colonel Jefferson, 136
DuPont Company, 116
DuPont's Deep-Water Point station, 118
DuPont's Gibbstown, New Jersey, 117
DuPont's Tacoma, Washington plant, 117

E

Edison Cement, 122
Edison, Thomas, 95
Egypt, 33, 34, 35, 36, 56, 68, 70, 71, 72, 73, 75, 77, 79
Eighth Air Force, 134, 135, 136, 165
El Mercurio, 193
Enki, 68
Exodus, 35

F

Ferdinand, Franz, 83
Foo Fighter, 163, 169
Forrestal, James Vincent, 132, 207
Fort Stevens, 151
Fort, Charles, 104
Friedman, Stanton T., 137

G

Garden of Eden, 25, 30, 67
Ghost Rockets, 185, 186, 187
Gordon, Cyrus H., 40
Great Pyramid, 57
Greece, 33, 34, 35, 39, 40, 68, 75
Greek Dark Ages, 37
Gudea, 42, 44

H

Hagley's Yard, 117
Hall, Michael D., 112
Hart, Will, 61
Harwood, Jeremy, 153
Henry, Bill, 156
Hercules, 61
Hittites, 80
Holcomb, Larry, 130
Homo Sapiens, 12, 13, 15, 19, 20, 22
Honoria, 50
Horus, 79
Howe, Bruce, 29

I

Imperial Japanese Army, 148
Ingersoll-Rand, 122
ISHTAR, 80
Isis, 79
Isle of Crete, 40
Israelites, 35, 36, 40, 41

J

Japanese submarine I-17, 149
Japanese Submarine, the I-25, 151
Jehovah, 57, 81, 82
Jerusalem, 43
Joseph, Frank, 113, 149, 161, 165, 167, 174, 196, 209
Joseph, Franz, 83

K

Kaiser Wilhelm, 83, 90
Kearns, David A, 191
King James Bible, 14, 81
King Solomon, 43
Knox, Frank, 154, 155
Kolchin, Gherman, 170

L

Lagash, 43
Landry, General Robert, 133
League of Nations, 89, 90
Legions of Rome, 50
Lenin, 66
Little America IV, 191, 192
Los Angeles Herald Express, 157
Los Angeles Times, 156, 157, 197
Lowery, R. L., 99

M

Maloney, Mack, 46, 63, 149, 164, 179, 186, 188, 199
Marcel, Jesse, 134, 137, 138
Marshall, Georgia C., 129, 130, 155
McClelland, J. H., 160
McMullen, General Clements,, 136
Meshach, 47
Messerschmitt 163A *Komet*, 172
Minoans, 35, 40
Morgan, J.E., 124

Moses, 43, 57
Mount Olympus, 75
Mycenaean, 35
Mystery airships, 93

N

Napoleon, 33
Neanderthal, 15, 16, 17, 18, 19, 20, 21, 23, 25, 26, 41
Nephilim, 61
New Literary Observer, 171
New Mexico, Roswell, 4, 73, 93, 127, 134, 137, 154, 201, 207, 208

O

Operation Highjump, 189, 191, 194, 196
Operation Majestic, 132, 133, 210
Operation Majestic 12, 136
Osiris, 79

P

Pearl Harbor, Hawaii, 147
Petrie, Flinders. *See* Petrie, Sir William
Petrie, Sir William, 74
Pope Leo I,, 50
Portsmouth Naval Shipyard, 112, 115
Prehistoric Investigations in Iraq Kurdistan, 29
prophet Ezekiel, 43
Prophet, Elizabeth Clare, 48

R

Ramey, General Roger, 134, 136
Ramses II, 80
Randle, Kevin D, 160, 168
Reitsch, Hanna, 172
Rendlesham Forest, 73

Rickenbacker, Captain Eddie, 110
RNN *Tromp*, 179
Rockefeller Museum, 74
Romanoff Family, 65
Rome, 33, 34, 45, 46, 49, 50, 51, 52, 68, 75
Ronner, John, 49, 52, 85
Roosevelt, President Franklin D., 129
Rosetta Stone, 34

S

Sabinski, Roman, 163
Sacramento Bee, 98
San Francisco Call,, 97
Sarnoff, General David, 187
Senusret II, 71
Set, the god of war, 79
Seti I, 70, 79
Shadrach, 47
Shanidar, 26, 28, 33
Shaw, Colonel H.G., 99
Sitchin, Zecharia, 12, 67, 210
Smith, Paul Blake, 127
Sobek, the Crocodile god, 78
Solecki, Ralph, 26
Solon, 35
Sophia, 83
Stevens, Henry, 173
Stimson, Henry, 159
Stonehill, Paul, 170
Sword, Terrenz, 157, 158

T

Task Force 68, 191, 192, 196
Taylor Wharton, 122
TESHUB, 80
The Annals of the World, 14
THE OCCULT CONNECTION, 4
Thutmosis III, 73
Tobias, 87
Trojan War, 78, 80
Trotsky, 66

Truman, President Harry S., 132, 133, 134, 188, 208, 209
Tulagi, 182, 183
Tulli Papyrus, 73
Tyre, 63

U

U.S. Air Force Historical Research Agency, 154
U.S. Fish and Wildlife Service, 19
United States Army Coast Artillery Association, 154
Ur, 43
Ur-Nammu, 43
USCGC Northwind, 190
USS Brownson, 190, 195
USS Burton Island, 190
USS Cacapon, 190
USS Canisteo, 190
USS Currituck, 190
USS *Helm*, 180, 181
USS Henderson, 190
USS Merrick, 190
USS Mount Olympus, 190
USS Philippine Sea, 189
USS Pine Island, 190
USS Sennet, 190, 196
USS Yancey, 190
Ussher, Archbishop, 14

V

Vander Ploeg, Dirk,, 156
Von Richthofen, Baron Manfred, 110
Von Zeppelin, Count Ferdinand, 105

W

Waitzrik, Peter, 110, 111
Watson, Nigel, 121
Wesley, John, 49
Wiles, Marvin, 157

Wilson, Woodrow President, 90
Wood, Robert M., 210
World War I, 83, 89, 103, 110, 127, 132, 139, 149
World War II, 89, 90, 96, 135, 139, 145, 147, 153, 163, 175, 181, 182, 183, 184, 185, 186, 195, 196, 197, 207

Z

Zeuner, Fredrick Everard, 31
Zeus, 60, 61, 78
Zhelaginova, Gennady, 170

www.ingramcontent.com/pod-product-compliance
Lightning Source LLC
Chambersburg PA
CBHW071853110526
44591CB00011B/1399